# To Me It's Wonderful

# Ethel Waters

# To Me It's Wonderful

*I'm His Precious Love*
*Ethel Waters*

With an Introduction by

Eugenia Price and Joyce Blackburn

Harper & Row, Publishers

New York, Evanston, San Francisco, London

TO ME IT'S WONDERFUL. Copyright © 1972 by Ethel Waters. All rights
reserved. Printed in the United States of America. No part of this book
may be used or reproduced in any manner whatsoever without written
permission except in the case of brief quotations embodied in critical
articles and reviews. For information address Harper & Row, Publishers,
Inc., 49 East 33rd Street, New York, N.Y. 10016. Published simul-
taneously in Canada by Fitzhenry & Whiteside Limited, Toronto.

LIBRARY OF CONGRESS CATALOG CARD NUMBER: 76-183634

Printed for World Wide Publications by special arrangement with Harper & Row
Publishers, Inc.

To
my precious child
Billy Graham
and
my entire Team family

## Introduction by
## Eugenia Price and Joyce Blackburn

This is Ethel Waters' own book, set down basically in her own words. Neither of us felt for one minute as though we were writing a book *for* her. We simply shared the tremendous experience of a great life relived and assisted in giving that experience form. Miss Waters had made copious notes. She knew exactly what she wanted told; exactly the impact she wanted the book to make on her readers. She knew exactly how the book would end. Ours was the unique privilege of being with her during the "telling."

We have both been rabid Waters fans since we were teen-agers. Neither of us has missed one of her performances when we could help it. We have known of her and loved her through the years as an artist whether she was interpreting a song or a starring role in the theater. It came as no surprise to us when our research turned up the fact that the most influential critics of the fifties considered Ethel Waters, along with Helen Hayes, Lynn Fontanne, and Katherine Cornell, the four top-ranking actresses in the world of American drama. It did come as a surprise to learn that so many who follow Miss Waters now, as she sings of her devotion to Jesus Christ, do not know this.

It is characteristic of this woman who deals in realities *not* to have traded on past greatness in order to convince her new admirers. The evidence is a matter of record. "Mom" did not turn to God, did not begin singing with Billy Graham's Crusades because she was "through" on the professional stage. Far from it. The recording of her famous one-woman show, popular at that time, remains a spellbinder because of her multifaceted technique and emotional range. But she does not need to live on past glory. Rather, she revels in knowing that her present audiences love her for *herself* and for the truth she communicates.

One of our reasons for assisting Miss Waters with *To Me It's Wonderful* was our desire to let her "new family" know the stature former achievements have given her, and as a consequence, what her decision to follow her Saviour really meant to her. On the other hand, we wanted those who did know her in show business to learn what she is like now.

Her hundreds of records are all collector's items; thousands of theatergoers still keep her playbills among their most valued possessions; some of the photographs reproduced in this book are priceless. Still, here is a lady in her seventy-sixth year, with a wider, equally enthusiastic "new" audience, embarked on the one career which has ever fulfilled *her* as a human being. Long-time fans are as devoted as ever. We know of hundreds who follow her everywhere there is a Graham Crusade just for a glimpse of Mom—a thrilling, treasured chance to hear her again—even for a few moments.

One of Mom's favorite young friends, Mr. George Finola, well-known for his association with the New Orleans Jazz Museum, told us of having arranged his schedule in order to drive from New Orleans to Baton Rouge when he learned Mom would sing there with the Graham Team. "The traffic was unbelievable," George said. "I fought it all the way, and when I reached the area of the Crusade, it grew more congested. I knew Mom would be on first and man, how I hurried! At last I found a place to park my car, and as I *ran* across the huge lot toward the arena, out over the loudspeakers came that glorious voice. It was Mom, just moving into the last phrase of 'Sparrow.' I ran faster, waving my arms and shouting, 'Wait, Mom, don't finish, Mom—I'm coming! Please wait!' "

We understand this. We feel the same way about her. We will never forget the hours spent with Miss Waters in her apartment in Los Angeles where she sits in a comfortable swivel chair looking out from the room-high windows. Converging down the hills is the city traffic, but inside it is quiet. Surrounding her are mementos, awards, photographs, fresh flowers from admirers, a grand piano littered with mail. "My nest," she calls it.

When we left, she warned, "You babies will miss me." She was right. We did. We couldn't wait for her to visit us two months later. And few nights go by that we don't play at least one of Mom's great albums.

The ultimate nature of this intuitive, wise-with-living, lovable, childlike, contradictory, passionate, thoroughly Christian artist cannot be captured between the covers of any book. As with a musical pitch—"I can hit it or bend it"—her moods are many, quick-changing, but she is peaceful. Her confidence in Jesus Christ is real. So is their companionship. In these pages you will find what has most meaning to Ethel Waters, herself, today. When you've finished, you will miss her too, as we do. But happily, we're all her "children" now and if, like us, you're convinced that there *is* "a cabin in the sky," you will find your solace, as we found ours, in knowing that one day we can count on being with Mom and with Mom's Lord for always.

# Part One

It was in the late fifties—spring of 1957—and I stood leaning into the curve of the piano on the stage of a Broadway theater, nearing the end of another of my one-woman shows, billed *An Evening with Ethel Waters.*

Intermission didn't rest me. I was by then too bulky to sit down once I was standing up. I left the stage only when I had to, because walking was such an effort. My ability and experience as an actress had been getting me through those one-woman performances for a long time, both in Los Angeles, where I owned my home, and in other cities around the country. I was too fat to breathe the way a singer has to. The last time I had been on a scale, I weighed in at 350 pounds. But I could still stand through those shows by leaning against a grand piano. I was called a "star," but being a star was to me just a nice way of saying I was a servant to my public. Not once in the then almost fifty years as a performer had I ever held back anything.

That night, with my precious Reginald Beane accompanying me, I had again given them all I had, and Reggie, as always, had supported me with all he had, and we had kept it moving. Reggie and I had worked together for over twenty years, and, through still another one-woman show, we were working our way to the concluding number, "Cabin in the Sky."

As always, the audience was with us, laughing at my ad libs, digging Reggie's great piano. Although I never judged my own performance by applause, the people that night had been "with me" all the way. I could feel that they loved me. Many of the older ones had followed me down through the years, because they applauded the minute I went into "Dinah," which I had introduced back in 1925. The same with "Stormy Weather" and "St. Louis Blues." They knew I had, with Duke Ellington, introduced Harold Arlen's "Stormy Weather" at the Cotton Club in Harlem and that I had been the first woman ever to sing professionally W. C. Handy's "St. Louis Blues." Exhausted as I was, those people out there were with me. Still respecting me. Still stirring my own heart, so that when I called them "children," I meant it. They were my children. All the children I ever had. Giving me all the love they had for the time I was singing to them; but once the show ended I knew I'd just take a cab back to my hotel and be alone again.

They clapped and shouted and cheered after I finished "Cabin in the Sky," and I stood there, the back of my gown wet with perspiration, with every breath becoming more difficult waiting for their applause to die down so I could—once more—begin the chorus of the song for which I was most famous.

> I sing because I'm happy,
> I sing because I'm free . . .

For the first two lines Reggie let me go it alone a cappella as I'd done in my most successful legitimate play, *The Member of the Wedding*. But that night in 1957 I needed the sure touch of Reggie Beane's hands on the keyboard to get me through. He moved under the melody line subtly at first, then filling, holding me up as I went on to—

> Why should I feel discouraged?
> And why should the shadows come?
> Why should my heart be lonely,
> Away from heaven and home?

> For Jesus is my portion,
> My constant friend is He,
> For his eye is on the sparrow
> And I know He watches me.

Ever since the long Broadway run of *The Member of the Wedding* when that old song had become associated with me in the mind of the public, I'd used it as my final encore. But the song meant more to me than just the association with *Member*. I had been singing it since childhood and it had sustained me for all of my life. Somehow I knew I'd get enough strength from it— enough to finish my concert with a real, pulsing closeness to my audience; praying in my heart that someone—maybe just one of them—would believe me when I said at the end—

> And children, I know—oh, how *I* know—He watches *we*!

Oh, I'd been hittin' them with a solid beat off and on all evening. I'd broken their hearts just before intermission, and my own right along with theirs, as I poured myself into my interpretation of "Supper Time," the song of a woman, a mother, whose husband had just been lynched. Irving Berlin had heard me sing "Stormy Weather" at the Cotton Club back in 1933, and he signed me, the first colored performer in an all-white cast for a Broadway show, to sing "Heat Wave" and "Supper Time" in his production *As Thousands Cheer*. Those two songs couldn't be more opposite in mood, in emotional range, and they took versatility. I was famous for that—versatility.

That night the audience had cried through "Supper Time," then I had them laughing, like when I shouted after finishing "Am I Blue?"—"I know I'm *fat*—but am I blue?" I didn't need to ask. I was both fat and blue and nobody knew it better than sixty-one-year-old Ethel Waters. And so I sang "Sparrow" for myself as well as for them.

Well, I stood for the long ovation. Reggie kept playing. They kept applauding and calling out that they loved me. I was surprised when I heard the Monmouth-Evergreen album of that night's performance. During that ovation, tired as I was, I had hummed—not knowing I was being recorded—an octave higher than I would have dared try if I'd known anyone was listening! It's unbelievable. It really is. My old pipes were too rusty to have soared way up there without some kind of help from outside. The help came from singing "Sparrow." From the One I sang about when I sang "Sparrow"—my precious Saviour.

I was all worn out, but could still hold an audience—just like in the early days of recording when Tommy and Jimmy Dorsey and Eddie Lang and Benny Goodman and Rube Bloom and Manny Klein, great boys—all of them—used to cancel their own dates sometimes to work with me. I'd done it all. Starred in glamorous musicals and movies and plays. I was the people's artist. Miss Ethel Waters. Now I was also their big, fat, comforting Mama image, who could—even as old and fat as she was—still be counted on to make them laugh and cry and forget their troubles for a little while. I had always gone out there in the lights wanting to give *them* happiness. So I closed with "Sparrow," praying that someone might find the comfort the song always gave me.

When Reggie and I left the stage at last, not a man or a woman that filed out of that theater needed comfort more than Ethel Waters needed it. My baby, Reggie, helped me squeeze into a taxi and saw me to my suite at the Empire Hotel in Manhattan, told me I was as great as ever, laughed off my thanks for the wonderful job he had done for me, and we hugged good-night. Maybe it would be good-by for awhile, because soon as I filled one more engagement in June and handled some business in New York, I would be flying back to my home in Los Angeles. When and if another big date came along, I'd be sending for Reginald Beane. Since the death of my other great accompanist and dear friend, Pearl Wright, many years before, it had always been Reggie I sent for when anything big came along. The boy was and is like my own son. I love him.

I walked to the window of my empty hotel suite.

Outside, down on the sidewalk, staggering along with their arms linked, I saw two Skid Row bums. Those two reeling along down there were drunk—but at least they had each other. They were together. I, Ethel Waters, the celebrity, was all by myself.

Alone and troubled.

Afraid, too, in a way. Afraid that I might never learn how to live with myself weighing 350 pounds. All my life I had been slender. My family was slender. My mother, Louise, was tall and big-boned like me, but never fat. My grandmother, Sally Anderson, rest her soul, was a slight, frail woman and also my aunts and my sister, Genevieve. And, suddenly, almost without my realizing it, I had piled on so much weight that I didn't know how to handle myself. You know, if you're born fat and stay fat, you don't know anything else. You handle it. You at least are used to being able to move your body around wherever you go. But worse than the handicap of forcing myself, a good part of my professional career had suffered because of it. You see, after the Broadway run of 501 performances as Berenice Sadie Brown in *Member,* and after the movie version in 1955, I had made good money regularly by playing Berenice Sadie Brown in stock performances all over the country. I closed the second act of *Member* holding a young girl on my lap and singing "Sparrow." Finally it became clear to me that I was going to have to stop playing Berenice Sadie Brown because I didn't have any lap left!

Oh, I could still do my one-woman shows and television guest appearances if my energy and strength permitted me to travel. But after *Member,* no matter what engagement I accepted, I would always be asked to sing "His Eye Is on the Sparrow." It was as though people got some comfort from hearing me sing that song. And I pray that they really did.

But you see, there's a lot about my life people don't understand. Even those that read my book which was published while *Member* was having its big Broadway run. The book was called *His Eye Is on the Sparrow.* A title like that would naturally make the play-going public think of me, but it went deeper than that. In fact, that song almost kept me out of Carson McCullers' play, *The Member of the Wedding!*

I've always been a person to know her own mind. I haven't understood myself—still don't—I'm complex, but I know what I think and what I believe. And in spite of the fact that I knew I could use the money and longed to be a part of another Broadway performance, I came near not taking the role of Berenice Sadie Brown in *Member* at all. When asked if I wanted the part I informed Bob Whitehead, the producer—a young man I liked very much—to let Harold Clurman, the director, and Carson McCullers, the author, know that the character of Berenice Sadie Brown, as Mrs. McCullers had drawn her, would not do for me. I said I've known colored women like Berenice Sadie Brown all right. Women who cuss and are downright nasty. I didn't question that Carson had done a good job of a certain kind of woman, but that woman wasn't me. Then, too, there was no God in the play. I would not, *would not* do the part unless it could be changed. I repeated that I could use the money, but that there was no chance the way it stood.

In spite of my objections, Bob Whitehead said he would call me when he got back from Denver in three days. You see, he wanted me to come to New York to talk with all of them about what I *would* agree to do. So, and I have to laugh now when I remember all this, I said to him, all right, he could call me back and if—*if* my phone hadn't rung offering me another job, I'd come and talk. Do you know, that telephone didn't even jangle? And I prayed. Oh, I prayed it would ring! Even if I'd had a call for just one night—one gig—I'd have never even talked about the part of Berenice Sadie Brown.

But since the phone played dead, I went to New York and in Bob Whitehead's home a scene took place I'll never forget. When I saw they wanted me enough to let me tone down the part from the way Carson had written it, I brought up the matter of the second act song. The song was originally supposed to be a Russian lullaby. I had never heard tell of a colored woman, especially from Georgia, who had ever sung a Russian ditty to a child! At first I thought Carson would stick in her heels on this. But finally—and she was sitting across the room from me in a big chair—she looked at me a long time with her big, sad eyes, then asked, "What song *would* you sing?"

I told her I had just the song. That I'd sung it all my life. She asked if I'd sing it right then.

I said Yes, I'd sing it, but that they might as well be ready for the mention of one Name that set some people's teeth on edge. The name of Jesus. I let them know that if I sang the verse to the song I wanted to do, I'd pronounce His name with all the love and tenderness I possessed. I did add that if they'd compromise—meet me halfway—and let me sing my song, I'd even be willing to omit that verse and sing only the chorus.

Carson McCullers looked at me again for a long time, rubbed out a cigarette in an ash tray, and said, "Will you sing it all—now, please?"

I started to sing, right there where I was sitting, and went all the way through "His Eye Is on the Sparrow."

When I finished, including the verse with the name of Jesus in it, there was a long silence in that room, except that Carson McCullers had crossed the room and was in my lap, crying.

Why all these memories came back to me as I looked out my window at the Empire Hotel I don't know, but even more than usual, singing "Sparrow" that night had stirred something deep inside me.

Remember, this was spring of 1957. I hadn't been able to play my version of Berenice Sadie Brown often, due to my size. I still missed young Brandon De Wilde who played the little boy, John Henry, in the Broadway production, and I suppose I will never

stop missing my precious, adorable child, Julie Harris, who played
Frankie in the big run of *Member*. For some reason, "Sparrow"
had brought them all back to me. I remembered the various TV
and radio talk shows Julie and I had done together when that
darling girl gave so much—too much—credit to what I'd done for
her in *Member*. It was her first big chance and she played Frankie
so beautifully, she has had top billing ever since. But I've searched
my mind—I searched my mind that night alone in my hotel room—
I still search my mind, trying to think what it was I could have
done for Julie to help her, except to love her. And oh, I didn't have
no choice about loving her. It was the same as if I'd borned her.
We loved each other on sight. It was like sparks. Sometimes when
she'd be so tired, she'd be worried about her voice being hoarse
and I'd tell her not to fret—not to use all her energy doing what
the rehearsal director was telling her to do—just to take it easy, be
natural, and Jesus would take care of her voice—that she only
sounded hoarse to herself. I remembered, too, that other times during the long, hard run of the play, when at the end of the second
act she got on my lap, she would relax so much I'd have to pressure
her a little to kind of rouse her so she'd be ready to come in on
the end of "Sparrow." Julie and I were close. For my birthday,
she gave me a cherished family heirloom—a cross set with dia-
monds which I had made into a ring. People are always asking
where they can buy one, but this is a treasure from my beloved
Julie Harris.

I can't think of anything I really did to help her. Maybe it was
the song itself. And me singing it the way I did with my whole
heart because of what it had always meant to me and because of
where I had learned it in the first place—way back when I was a
little girl. Long, long years ago—before I began to sing in colored
clubs as "Sweet Mama Stringbean" (they called me that because of
my "lissome and willowy form"!) for ten dollars a week; before
1927, when I had already made a batch of hit records and got my
first Broadway starring role in *Africana;* before ever Irving Berlin

heard me sing; before I co-starred with Beatrice Lilly on Broadway in 1935; before *Mamba's Daughters* and *Cabin in the Sky*. Before my starring role in *Pinky,* one of the movies I'd done.

"Sparrow" has always seemed to me to be almost *before* everything else. Maybe some people were surprised that for all those 501 times I sang it in *Member,* the audience was in tears, but it didn't surprise me. That song was the marrow in my bones. Even when I was a child it had given me spiritual comfort and that was long before Carson McCullers or Bob Whitehead or Julie Harris had been born.

I was too tired that night at the Empire Hotel even to hum it as these things went through my mind, but "Sparrow" can go through your mind without a sound being made. It can comfort you, but it didn't comfort me that night. Its familiar strains seemed to tear me up. To make me restless.

There I was, trapped in all that fat, so I couldn't even walk the floor. Troubled. *Troubled.* Even the usually cheering memory of when my beloved grandmother, Sally Anderson, used to call me in from play in the streets of Chester, Pennsylvania, and make me pump the old organ and sing "Sparrow" to her, didn't help. That night I couldn't muster a smile remembering.

I was a tall, overgrown child, the same as my mother, Louise, was always big for her age. I wasn't fat then, just big-boned, tall. I shot up too fast ever to know the child joy of being comforted and patted and held on anybody's lap. There weren't any laps big enough to hold me! Louise, which is what I called my own mother, was only twelve years older than me and she didn't have any desire to hold me. She was too ashamed of the way I had been borned. My grandmother, whom I called Mom, couldn't hold me. "Run on and play, you're too big." But I knew she loved me. And oh, how I loved her!

Alone that night in New York, "Sparrow" set up such a longing in me, I thought I might die. It was like for the first time, I realized how almost every part of my long, sometimes tragic, some-

times successful life—the funny parts when I couldn't help laughing and the sorrowful parts when I laughed to block off the tears—
the parts lived out in the narrow, dark alleyways of Philadelphia
and the parts lived out under the bright lights of Broadway—had
all been somehow tied into that old song, because "Sparrow" had
always been such a part of me.

I had known it almost all of my sixty-one years, and I knew
exactly where I learned it first. You see, if Louise wanted to hurt
Mom who tried to keep me close to her wherever she was working
in service, Louise would snatch me away or send me to my Aunt
Ide's to live awhile or hire me out. I was boarded to and fro all
my childhood days, but I'll never forget Aunt Ide's neighbors, the
folks who lived back of her house. Their name was Bell and what
a wonderful family they were! Dr. Bell, the father, was the
preacher in a little church nearby. He had ten children and I loved
them all. Well, the Bells used to take me to their church—a teeny
little church with benches running across almost from wall to wall.
That was where I first learned "Sparrow." That was where I
learned most of the hymns I now know. I can still hear that hand-
ful of the faithful, singing, while somebody pumped the wheezy
organ to lead ahead in that long, slow beat:

> Why should I feel discouraged?
> Why should the shadows come?
> Why should my heart be lonely,
> Away from heaven and home?

That night in New York tears ran down my cheeks. I stopped
the memory of the song. I *knew* I felt discouraged. I *knew* why
the shadows had come. I *knew,* oh, I *knew* why my heart was lonely
and that story also went back to my childhood. When I was twelve
years old and attending a children's revival meeting at another
little colored church in Chester, nearer where I was born on Front
Street—the railroad used to run up and down between Front and
the river—they sang "Sparrow" in this church too. I loved to

listen, but not to join in. I didn't belong to this particular church I'm talking about, because like my grandmother, Sally Anderson, I considered myself a Catholic. I had gone to a Catholic school in Philadelphia for awhile once, but I went to the other Protestant church for the August quarterly meeting like everyone else. Partly I went because the food was so good, *and* the preaching. Oh, that pastor was a preachin' man and he wasn't regimental about how he conducted the services, either. If the Spirit moved you and you wanted to shout, why you shouted! He wasn't a shouter himself, but he had *fire*. You know, sometimes you can say a word a certain way that makes other people want to shout. And another time, you can make them want to cry. Lots of people don't understand when tears run down the cheeks of folks in a church that they're happy! They say—crazy. Funny. Peculiar. But nobody thinks it's funny if those girls that win beauty contests stand there with their crowns askew, lookin' kind of silly—cryin'! Why? What's the difference? They're happy and they cry because they're happy. Can't God's people cry because they're happy too?

Oh, I tell you, that preachin' man back in Chester at the August meeting affected folks. Made them cry for joy or made them cry over their sins. I still recall the twelve-year-old overgrown skinny girl named Ethel Waters, who *knew* in her heart that she felt uneasy about God. I had gone to my grandmother's church, but I wasn't peaceful in my rebellious young heart. I had no trouble going to church on Sundays and heading up a street gang on Monday. That is, I had no trouble over it *until* I heard that preachin' man in Chester.

Stretched on the couch in my hotel suite, too tired to undress and get to bed, I was hearkening back to that Quarterly meeting— remembering how I was unable to stay away, still not feeling I was good enough to be there. And every night, the other youngsters would get up and troop down to the old wooden mourner's bench to get saved. I wouldn't go, because I was smart. I was going to think it all out *my way*. After all, I was mostly all right. I couldn't see I needed much. Wasn't my grandmother a staunch Catholic and my mother a stauncher Protestant? Didn't I have both fronts covered?

Every night until the last night, the preacher had always asked them that wanted to come, to put up their hands. I'd never put mine up and I'd never stood up. But he fooled me that last night. He changed it around so that he asked everybody to come down who wasn't an out-and-out Christian! And so, without understanding much about why, I knew I *had* to go.

I went down and stood by that mourner's bench and the preacher talked to all of us and he talked to me and then we all got down on our knees—me too. But reluctantly. And I thought, well, I'm here, I'd better say something to God. So, I said under my breath, "What am I down here for?" Now, one thing I'd always known—I learned it in Catholic confession—was that God and Jesus want honesty. I was sure Jesus knew that I didn't really know why I was there. Jesus *knew* I didn't know what to ask or do. God knew it too. And I knew they both knew it.

They went on with the meeting that night with me on my knees at the mourner's bench getting nowhere. When it was over, I was what they called "under conviction." I just hadn't "come through." That was another term they used when a person got up off his knees unsatisfied in his heart. The next night I went down front again. Nothing happened then, either. All the rest of the people were jumping up like Russian dancers—jumping up and down all over the place. I guessed their knees must have hurt from all that kneeling. The floor was hard! As hard as the benches. There weren't any plush cushions around anywhere for sitting or for kneeling. I knew I was sorry if I'd done anything terribly wrong, but I didn't know what to do about it. I honestly didn't know how to "come through." And I wouldn't pretend. The preacher extended that service for me, but nothing happened. I still didn't know what to ask God for or what to do. And those dear, sweet women and men, they prayed and prayed for me. Every night I was down there again, on my knees at that mourner's bench, but still nothing happened.

Then, on the very last night of the meetings, I went down once more, and I said, "Lord, I *got* to know *someway*. If I don't know You someway, I'm not ever comin' back!"

This time . . . He let me know.

Not now, as I tell you this story, nor that night in my New York hotel room back in 1957, could I remember getting up off my knees. I don't remember getting up. But, as the song goes, "He touched me." *He touched me.*

Those folks in that little church knew of my need and they were overjoyed. I was one of the worst brats on the street. Over and over I'd heard people say, "That Louise's daughter, Ethel, is one of the worst kids in Chester." I don't care now who knows that I was a ring leader of street gangs and street life in the slums. I only knew that night when I got up off my knees, it didn't matter no more that I'd been bad. It still doesn't matter. That's gone. People, a certain kind of people, just plain want you to tell them all the foul stuff. They're curious. So I'm levelin'. Some people want your guts, although they don't want to spill theirs. But I can tell you that I knew that night at age twelve that when God's in your heart, you can puke and it's okay, because He knows it all already! So, then and now, I *tell* about myself. Maybe somebody else can vomit too and feel better.

That night back in 1957 in a lonely hotel room I could still hear those saints telling me that when I got up at last from the mourner's bench, it showed all over me what had happened. It was wonderful! Instead of pulling back, protecting myself, trying to hide my shyness with big talk and filthy words, instantly, I had freedom to get up in church and just talk about Jesus. I could talk and I could pray—out loud, too. And going to be among Jesus' own people was the only thing that interested me. I loved them. I loved to hear the singing. The little church was the only place I felt at home. The only place.

All of that memory still gave me hope, I found, at sixty-one, but a sorrow was there too in me. The now familiar, burdensome sorrow I'd carried around for almost fifty years since that beautiful night when the peace and the light and the happiness of heaven were in me and around me. Through every long year between, I had dragged the sorrow because of a tragic thing that had happened. You see, there was a girl in that church—a kind of would-be high society girl—and she was very jealous of me. I guess jealousy is the worst feeling you can have. It happens to be one of life's most destructive sins. I've never been blind jealous of anybody. Not even of other entertainers. I could always manage to say, "I don't like her, but she sure can sing!" Or, "I don't like him, but he sure looks sharp in his clothes." Somehow I've always been able to do that and I'm glad. Nothing warps and eats on you like jealousy.

Well, we younger ones back in Chester were working on some kind of an affair to raise money for the church and this girl picked a fuss with me. Now, I've always had a habit of saying things too quickly. (I still have to try and check myself and to this day, I laugh and say that's one good reason why I live alone!) But this girl picked her fuss and I honestly didn't know why. Anyway, right in the vestibule of the church, she started this argument and it was my first confrontation following my conversion. I'd always been able to come out on top of any confrontation. I could sling words so sharp they'd cut you through. I could enforce what I said, too. I had tried to keep out of bad arguments even before my conversion to Jesus Christ, because I just didn't know my own physical strength. I was so strong and so violent as a child, that I didn't want anyone to touch me for fear I couldn't restrain myself. If you hit me, I was willing to go all out to do you in. And I'd have no remorse either. Not if you touched me first, see. In those days, before I knew Jesus, if you provoked me I was only sorry if I didn't finish you off!

In that church vestibule, I stood face to face with my first big temptation as a Christian. I knew what I could do to that girl. And it was worse, because I honestly didn't know what she had against me. I stood there kind of trembling, and I said, "Look here, I don't even want to talk to you!" And I started to walk away from her, to get out, but being me, and prone to quick statements, I snapped on my way to the door, "Aw, gal, I ain't payin' you no mind— you're just breedin'!" Right away, I thought: What made me say a thing like *that*?

The next thing I knew, she was after me, clawing my face. She wore long, pointed fingernails and I can still feel them tearing big, deep gashes in my cheeks. Fortunately, the other girls held me so I couldn't get to her, or I guess I would have torn her to pieces.

At sixty-one, the memory of that fight was still so clear I could remember the old kerosene stove—the way it smelled when I went to the house later that evening. I didn't speak to anybody, but went to my little box of a room and cried and prayed all night. I was just past twelve years old, but my heart was broken. I knew that next Sunday would be Communion. I had looked forward to partaking of the Lord's Supper, but I knew now I couldn't. I wouldn't. I wouldn't touch it. I said, "Nope, I hate that girl, Lord, and I can't do it."

I never went back to the church again.

I knew I had hate in my heart and that wasn't fair to God. I tried, but I couldn't get rid of it and so I never went back.

For awhile, I used to wait around on street corners intending to get even with that uppity girl, to beat her good for messin' up my face. But the only satisfaction I had was that I found out later I had told the truth about her in the church vestibule without knowing it! She *was* pregnant.

I never went back to church and I started right in jiggin', shimmyin', singin' any kind of songs I liked and everything like that. The people from the church would come to talk to me and I appreciated that they did. I wasn't against them! Not at all. I just knew that I had let the Lord down and I couldn't help myself. I'd say, "Oh, dear Lord, I didn't do nothin' to that girl and look what she did to me. I can't forgive her, Lord! I can't. *I can't.*"

Down through nearly fifty years, I never sang again in a church. Oh, I sang. I sang my way up and up to the top in show business, but in spite of the "fame and fortune" that came to me, I guess you could say that "Sparrow" haunted me. It seemed sometimes that I could still hear them singing it the way they sang it in that little church, and I sang it wherever I had a chance. Like that night back in 1957, as the final encore number on my one-woman show. But my sorrow was always there even when I did.

The loneliness for that wonderful *certainty* of God I had the night I got up off that hard floor at the mourner's bench at age twelve, never left me. No success, no high fees, no awards, nothing —*nothing*—ever measured up to what I had lost with Jesus. I still believed in Him. I prayed. I read my Bible and cried out for help in my times of trouble. I asked His help before every performance. But with all the curtain calls I took, with all the applause and rave reviews and custom-designed clothes and jewelry—riding around in my big Lincoln—I still felt lonely for Jesus. Still missed the joy, the security, the peace of that shining, beautiful thing we'd once had—together.

It was really late, so I hauled myself up off that sofa and got ready for bed. I turned out my light and did what I'd been doing since the early fifties. For years, at night, I'd hunt around the radio dial, hoping to find a real preachin' man to listen to. To quiet my confused, bitter, lonely heart. Hoping against hope that even for a few minutes I might recapture some of that feeling of closeness to Jesus I'd missed all those years.

By then, I'd heard many colored preachers. White preachers, too, but still I'd search that radio dial. Now, I hadn't always loved white people, I can tell you. I'll be candid, I did *not* love them. In fact, I just didn't like them—period. Of course, I was wrong. Just like some whites don't like colored. I understand that. I didn't even like *light* people either because my grandmother, rest her soul, hated my white grandmother Lydia, my father's mother, over what she did to my mother when she refused to let my father, John Waters, claim me. My grandmother didn't ask him to marry my mother or nothing like that, but she wanted it understood that my mother had not entered into their relationship of her own free will. That she had been raped. And so it was drilled into me that anybody who was "light" was just no good. If you were bright skinned, I hated you, because my grandmother had told me that.

When possible, I listened regularly to a young preacher named Billy Graham. This was long before I saw his picture. I had only heard him preach on the radio. And when I finally saw a picture of him, I thought, "Huh-uh! He's too good lookin'." Some of the preachers I knew about were also handsome and sharp looking, and from the tales I heard, most of them had kinda slipped around, you know. And then, to be honest, I wondered if white people could have the same zeal for God, Jesus, and the Bible that I'd seen. I'm just levelin' with you. These are the things that went warrin' around in my mind about Billy Graham for years! So I wondered about Billy Graham and yet I kept listening to him. There was just something. He kept getting across—to *me*. He wasn't full of Amens and always quoting what John Doe or Jane Smith said, or what anybody else said—this boy said, "The Bible says!" And "Jesus says!"

Even after all those years, you see, it was still Jesus I wanted. So many want to bypass Jesus. Oh, they'll bring God in every now and then, but they certainly make a big point of leaving Jesus out. I still loved and missed *Jesus,* and Billy Graham bore down on Jesus and I admired him for it.

Sure enough, that night after I got into bed, in a few minutes there was that now familiar voice preaching about Jesus. Billy Graham. I lay there propped up on my pillows and listened. I was still out in the world—a long way out—but I sat there and said, "Thank you, Jesus." Oh, boy, Billy was laying it off with so

...nd so, in his dynamic way, like only Billy can, just like
...ning!

Then they made an announcement when he finished that almost
rocked me out of bed. The Billy Graham Crusade was coming to
New York—to Madison Square Garden that very month of May!

I had meant to leave to go back to my own home in Los
Angeles just as soon as I found out about a possible short run
of *Member,* and finished up one more theater date and a few
remaining appearances with Tex McCrary and Jinx Falkenberg—
two lovely children whom I adore. Those two have been wonderful to me. For a long time they had invited me to appear on their
morning show. They'd let me sing anything I liked—and if I
forgot the words, I'd hum. Then people who treasured those old
songs would write in and send me the words. There was real
warmth to that Tex and Jinx program.

A few days later, around the middle of May, I was putting on
my TV make-up and Tex came by, ribbing me as usual. I should
have expected something like a loaded question from him that
day on camera and it came! Right out of the blue when we were
on the air just talking about first one thing and another, Tex
looked me in the eye and asked if I'd heard Ruth Graham inter-
viewed on TV the day before. I said I had, why? He didn't answer
my question, but went right ahead to ask me if I was planning to
attend the Crusade meetings. Not another soul knew that I had
been praying hard that the possible *Member* appearance would
fall through so I could go to the Crusade before I had to leave for
my home in Los Angeles. But I had been praying that and so I
told Tex, "Yes. At least I want to go. I hope I can." Next thing I
knew, Tex asked, "Ethel, what do you think it's going to do—
what do you think this Crusade is going to mean?" I said, "Tex,
it's going to be wonderful!" I told him I was *not* kidding, that I
thought it was going to be a terrific success. "What makes you
think so?" he asked. "Well," I answered, "for one thing, God
never sponsors a flop!"

I didn't stop there, either. I heard myself coming out with another statement I'd never even thought about before: "The Garden's not only going to be full, but the meeting will be extended!"

Now, this was me talking out of the clear blue and the Crusade hadn't even opened. But when I said it, I knew I believed it. I didn't know Billy Graham or anybody who would be involved in those meetings, but I knew that what I'd just said to Tex and Jinx was true! I'd been reading in the papers about how some Christians had been downgrading my Jesus and talking about Billy, not even wanting him to come to New York. So I took this chance to blow my big mouth, and at that moment I would have gone down swinging to defend the Crusade. And I wasn't supposed to be a Christian at all!

Tex and Jinx went on with the show, and when I got back to the hotel—and this is true as sure as I have to meet my Maker—there was a phone call from a member of the Crusade team, Lane Adams, wanting to know if Miss Ethel Waters would like some tickets to attend the opening meeting. I said I would gladly accept. When we hung up, I was mystified. For the first time I realized fully what I'd just said to millions of TV viewers on the Tex and Jinx show. I only knew it had come from my heart.

The Crusade office sent tickets to my hotel for the whole week—for me and nine friends—good ones in the loges where the seats were wider, thank heaven. Nothing, nothing could have kept me away. I said I was going just to see if this Billy Graham, this handsome blond, sharp-dressing "leading man" type, could possibly be for real. Although I was tired, nothing could have kept me away.

The night I dressed to go to the first Crusade meeting it seemed to me that ever since I had walked away from Jesus with hate in my heart, it had been autumn. In life we go through seasons—spring, summer, autumn, winter. Jesus didn't walk away from me. And I did still believe in Him, but through so many years of suc-

been autumn. Barren, lonely autumn. At that time, life
en more depressing for me. People asked me to talk about
y past. My past wasn't happy. My professional life wasn't happy.
It was highly successful, but it wasn't happy—for me. That's why
now, I don't like to be reminded of it. I gave happiness. I tried
always to give out happiness to my public, but that night autumn
closed in around me. The desolation of all my sixty-one years was
choking me when I went to Madison Square Garden to hear a
young preacher. I almost had stage fright. I was so—what I suppose you would have to call bewildered by my own suspense,
expectation. Yet all the time telling myself that Billy Graham just
couldn't be for real.

The old Madison Square Garden was certainly no strange place
to me. Off and on for years, I had appeared there in benefit shows
of one kind or another. All the top entertainers from Hollywood,
Broadway, and the better clubs would be on the bill with me to
raise money for some charity or foundation. Those VIP benefits
were all pretty much alike. Crowds would jam the gates till opening, then come streaming into the glare of the Garden's bright
lights, shoving to get to their seats. In no time at all, the air would
turn blue with smoke, and the noise—the din almost never let up.
There would be hollering and cussing backstage where we, the stars
were dressing, and out front the fans would yell and whistle and
stomp and applaud our acts. That whole scene was familiar to me.

But this night when I walked into the Garden, filling with
people, nothing was the same. It was quiet, you could hear the
murmur of the crowd, but there was nothing resembling noise. A
pale, soft blue light seemed to permeate the whole atmosphere,
soothing, comforting. Not smoke, light. We were shown the entrance where to my surprise they were expecting me.

When I walked in the Garden that first night, early, the choir
was singing "This Is My Story," one of the songs we used to sing
in the little church in Chester. Except for my friends who came in
with me, I didn't know a soul, but I never felt so welcome, so much

at home anywhere as I did right then. I was amazed at the transformation in the old Garden. I still am. I think about it yet. I couldn't get over the sense of friendship and love and quietness that God had spread over that big crowd of people. You don't get that anywhere else. I know. It is a real Christian feeling for people —one to another—and suddenly I had a deep hunger to be a part of it. True, I had known more than my share of the friendliness, the closeness among performers, especially if the show was a hit. And certainly, I had experienced more than one woman's share of admiration and acclaim from the public. But that doesn't last. You can take eighteen curtain calls one night, but if you play to an empty house the next night, you're as out of mind as yesterday's headlines.

We found our seats and I just sat there drinking it all in. Over and over to myself, I said, This is wonderful! This is just wonderful! Don't misunderstand me. I wasn't purified or anything like that—to me, it was just *wonderful*. The feeling I had. I didn't join in the singing. I didn't like to take part in community singing if you want to know the truth. Never had. In the days of my greatest popularity, what people couldn't understand about me and I couldn't understand about myself was that I've always been reticent. I'm shy. Nobody believes it, but it's still true! Because of my fame as I have to term it, I'm always judged by the kind of show person who's flamboyant. People always think I'm putting on an act. With me, being shy is not an act. Why, when I go to a theater, I sit in the back row and enjoy the thing! If I go in a place, I don't march down no aisle—no signifyin', no production, no grandstandin'.

I didn't sing with the choir or the congregation that first night at the Garden. I listened. Oh, how I listened! Our seats were some distance from Billy Graham. But how I clung to every word he said. And the more he said, the more I knew that what I felt when I first walked in was that my Lord was calling me—me, Ethel Waters, His child—to come on back home. It seemed like Billy Graham had come there to the Garden that night just to talk to

...w it then, but now I know that like Elijah, I was
...y a raven! (I have a dear friend in Philadelphia, named
...Donald, who calls me Elijah because she says I'm so strong
...impregnable. I call myself Elijah because I still need ravens to
feed me!) I had been so hungry down through those long years.
I had been missing spiritual food, missing my fulfillment, the
beautiful fulfillment I'd known the night God first touched me
back in the little church in Chester. I had been hungry and I had
been thirsty. Maybe I was eating myself half to death because I
was so spiritually hungry and thirsty. Drinking soda pop had been
no substitute for the cup of cold, living water I craved. There had
been that void, that emptiness which had never been filled since the
night He touched me when I was twelve years old. No one is ever
a loner by choice, but I couldn't find anybody who knew what to
do with all the love I needed to give. Nobody I could trust.

As I sat there in the Garden that night, I thought: *I'm not
satisfied even though I've always worn the things of the world like
a loose garment. You know, Jesus, that those things have never
been my real goal. Your grace let me achieve far beyond what
even I dreamed in the theater, Lord, and I wonder if you permitted
it because You knew fame and success had never been my big goal.
I've been amazed by all of it, Lord, but I never wanted it above
anything. I didn't. I never did. You know I still don't understand
what it is about me that makes people come to hear me sing and
see me act. I still don't understand about* artistry. *I can't grasp it.
I don't want to know. I'm lonesome, Lord. I'm lonesome.*

I sat through that first sermon listening to Billy Graham and
talking in my heart to Jesus that way, asking Him over and over—
how do I get back? How do I get back? I already believe. But, *how
do I get back?* Even with all the quietness and peaceful atmosphere
as I sat there in the Garden that night, I faced that my big problem
was that I wanted to love and get love back. I didn't want a man.
Don't misunderstand me, I'm a normal woman. But I'd been so
hurt. Really hurt and mistreated in my personal life by anyone I'd

ever really loved. I knew a lot of it had been my fault. Ethel Waters was so many-sided; it mixed everybody up. She was still that overgrown little girl looking for a lap to sit on—none of that had been changed by stardom. My professional life got in the way too, along with my being so hard to understand. No man wanted to be called Mister Waters! Looking back now, I can't say that I wouldn't have put a man before God, and He's a jealous God. I never birthed no children either. I lost two. I love children. They could have come before God with me, too. So I know He had some purpose. I was never an ornery woman. I am still just a human woman. I've been married, although I don't use a married name. Never have.

I've never cared what others thought of me. With me, it was always—just me. I never met the Joneses, so I don't have to worry and never did have to worry about keeping up with them. Maybe my life was affected by my mother being raped when I was conceived. I was never, never promiscuous. I was careful. Careful. On guard. And maybe that was part of the reason for my always having been so alone. Now I can see—and I tried to think it through that night at the Garden—that God did have a purpose. Maybe my loneliness was a blessing, because being so headstrong I wouldn't have found what I wanted anyway. What I wanted more than anything out of life was *understanding*. How I wanted somebody to understand me, to give me compassion and comfort! That night I faced up to the fact that I'd never had it from *anybody*. Ever since I'd been big enough to shift for myself, I've had to do it, take care of myself. Nobody else would look after Ethel. Just Ethel.

All of those things I weighed in my mind listening to Billy Graham preach that first sermon of the 1957 New York Crusade. I couldn't tell you a single thing he said in so many words. But as I listened to him preach and as I mulled my needs over in my heart before God, I recognized my confusion about so many things.

You see, in spite of my rebellious nature from the time I was

...ded then by poverty and all its vices—and long-
...ig enough to sit on—I had been in what you would
...il a religious environment at home. My precious grand-
...r, Sally Anderson, was a devout Catholic. My own mother,
whom I also called Momweeze, was a strict Protestant. I always felt
my grandmother loved me. Because I was not a child of love, because of the circumstances of my illegitimate birth, until much
later in my life I didn't receive love from my own mother. Yet,
looking back, I realized I had always sensed something different
in my mother's religion. Different than what my grandmother had.
What my mother had wasn't *seen,* but it was felt, and I used to
watch her and pity her when I was a child because her Christianity
was belittled. It wasn't accepted by the rest of the family. That
was the tragic side of my mother's life, because more than anything
else she wanted to do what I'm doing now—travel around and
sing and talk about Jesus. My grandmother and aunts used to tell
me that ever since she was a little girl, my mother had fervent
feelings about Christianity. Don't forget she had me when she was
a child of twelve! Too big for a girl her own age to play with, and
she would get in dutch if she played with somebody older because
she didn't know as much as they did yet. She was just too young
and slow-thinking. All big children's growth, mentally, isn't up to
their size. I thank God that my mind, my sense of values, seemed
to come up with my size. I was not a dumb child, but I can certainly
understand a child who has a seven-year-old mind and a fourteen-
year-old body! It's nice when you're a baby and everybody talks
about what a chubby, lovable tyke you are, but when you spring
up physically, you still maintain those childish traits and longings.
Though you'd better not hold onto them! People expect you to act
according to your size instead of your mind. The result is people
can be cruel, even when they don't mean to be.

Sitting there in the Garden, I pitied my mother, who by that
time had begun to show me some love and whom I *adored.* I pitied
her and I understood her as she had never been able to understand

me. I thought about how she had turned, in her rejection and her bitterness over my birth, to Jesus. I understood why she had seemed so fanatical about her Christianity. So pulled into herself. She was an inexperienced Christian, but God was all she had.

The Catholic influence in my life was strong too. *I learned from both.* But I was also confused by both, and as I listened to Billy Graham preach, I faced that confusion although he wasn't saying one word about either Protestants or Catholics. I had loved all my Catholic experience. Catholics believed in works, you might say, although I don't have the theological knowledge to explain the difference. I knew Catholics who brought poor children in and made them acquainted with the love of God. They weren't afraid to use the name of Jesus, either, those Catholics I knew. They would go right into the slums or anywhere and teach the love of Jesus. And they practiced it too! The nuns who taught me what little I was taught in the way of education practiced the love of Jesus Christ. I *know*. And they were the best psychiatrists. They really tried to help you solve your personal problems. The thing I noticed, though, at the age of twelve or so was that you can't *teach* fulfillment! It's as though you say, "I want a drink of water." Somebody says, "I don't have water, but here's some pop." So you drink pop. It doesn't satisfy. "What about some milk?" "Nope." Nothing quenches your thirst but water. Jesus Christ is the cup of water. Not for one minute do I say that Catholics aren't Christians! But the point is that Jesus seemed just as real to Momweeze at home, where I'd hear her talking to Him around the house, as in church. And that for me was important.

One thing the Catholic people taught me, that I'll revere and bless them for as long as I live, is honesty. They taught me that I had to be honest when I talked to the priest. This teaching helped me that night at the mourner's bench. It never occurred to me *not* to be honest with the Lord.

But, between my mother's staunch Protestantism and my grandmother's Catholicism, I was confused.

Sitting in that loge seat at the Garden, my confusion went far deeper than Catholicism or Protestantism. Nor was I fighting coming home to Jesus. I was not fighting Him. I wanted to be back with Him again all the way. Nobody had dragged me to that Crusade meeting. I went of my own accord. Eagerly, like a child. And I wanted, I longed to come home. But the confusion came here—I hadn't been in a church for so long, how could I understand the Mass (which was still in Latin then) or how could I ever figure out the difficult Protestant Bible? Remember, that was before they had the good plainer versions like now. Sitting there listening to Billy Graham, I wasn't fighting God or the Catholic or the Protestant churches. I was fighting my way through my own bewilderment about many things. My mixup inside was *personal.* It had to do with Ethel Waters herself.

Billy gave the invitation, and even if I hadn't been so big I needed help to get out of my seat, I wouldn't have gone forward. I already believed! And nobody in a back room needed to tell me that something inside my heart wasn't right. I knew that too. Even though I had never stopped for one minute—either praying or believing—something was missing, and nobody needed to point it out to me. I had tried, how I had tried, all through the years of my professional career to be a good Christian. You talk about works? I worked at it. I gave to charities even when I had to borrow the money. I supported my mother and different members of my family. I did everything I knew to do, but not once—not once, except when I walked into Madison Square Garden that night, had I even come close to feeling at peace with Jesus. I loved Him. I knew He loved me. I would tell my audiences right after I finished singing "Sparrow" that "He loves you—and so do I."

Everything Billy said registered with me, and the next night I was right back in that loge seat. The next night and the next and the next. I couldn't stay away. No one was pushing me. *I couldn't stay away.* Being as fat as I was, it took real effort to force myself into my clothes every night and get there. And it was always a long walk too, but I had to be there. I couldn't help myself. And each night when I'd go back to my suite at the Empire Hotel, I'd feel peculiar in a sort of way I couldn't explain. I knew I ought to be making reservations to go back to California. The possible engagement with a stock company of *Member* had fallen through. I had only one more theater date left to do—another one-woman show. That was coming up in less than a week. After that, I should get on my way home, because you see, my house had to be sold to make room for a freeway. I needed to be there to handle the sale. I had a girl named Floretta Howard working for me and she'd call me at night to ask, "When will you be back? The man was here wanting to know what your price is." I'd tell her I'd get there just as soon as I could. But all I really thought about was how many hours I'd have to get through before I could haul on my good clothes again and get back to hear Billy!

It remains one of the hardest things I've ever done, but when the time came for that one theater date, I kept it. The pay was $1,500, and it was either play or pay. I couldn't afford to pay out that kind of money right then, so I played. The first week of meetings ended, and Floretta was more and more upset with me every time I stalled about when I was coming home. Finally, she said, "Well, the man wants to know the name of your lawyer." I said, "Jesus." And by then, I meant it. I really did. In a strange and yet simple way, my life—even my business affairs—had come to be tied in with what I was finding in those meetings. Anyway, I didn't trust lawyers.

It seemed as though I just couldn't face leaving New York. Three times I made reservations back to Los Angeles and each time I canceled. All that mattered was that I make it for one more night to the Crusade. One more and then one more and one more. But by that time, I was getting tired of drumming up folks to go with me, so I called Lane Adams, the Crusade member who got me the first tickets. I had learned that Lane Adams was one of Billy Graham's Associate Evangelists, and by then he was joking about being my press agent. "I've got to come," I heard myself saying to him on the telephone, "but I'm not able to stand in that line and wait for a ticket. I'm just too heavy! My legs wouldn't stand that long." You see, I knew the line would be there by two in the afternoon, clean around the block. "Is there some way for me to get a pass?"

Lane Adams said I could join the choir.

I didn't answer him for a minute. Then I said, "But I'm not a churchgoer."

"That's all right, Miss Waters," he said. "If you want to join the choir, you certainly are welcome."

"But what I want," I said with a laugh, "is one of those buttons to get me inside! How can I lay my hands on a button?"

"By becoming a regular member of the choir. You come at three today, go through the entrance marked Choir and sign up. You'll get your button."

The last thing I wanted to do was to sing in that choir! I did hate group-singing. But if I had to say I'd sing in the choir in order to get into the meeting, then I'd do it. All I wanted was to get in without dropping dead in the line outside and without having to round up a whole gang of people each night. It was a trick. Jesus knew it. He also knew it was a lie when I said, "Fine, I'd love to become a member of your choir." I didn't mean to go near that choir.

But I had to go along with the protocol, and so I went meekly at three o'clock to the choir entrance, signed a card, and *got my button*. But this sweet lady named Maretta Campbell was right there ready to escort me to a seat in the alto section of the Crusade choir! I still have to whoop at myself when I remember that. You see, I wasn't counting on being *escorted*. I wasn't counting on singing in the choir at all. I just wanted that button so I could get in and then sit where I pleased. But God trapped me.

I was stuck, in more ways than one, believe you me. When I got in there where the choir sat, it didn't take long to see that if I managed to squeeze into one of those seats, I'd never manage to get out. So, a member of the team named Bill Brown found a special chair for me he thought would do fine. I tried it and the upshot was that poor Bill Brown had to saw off the outside arm so I'd fit—so my spill would be accommodated!

I still laugh so hard I can hardly tell it, but for the whole sixteen weeks of that Crusade with me in the choir, I was in suspension—you know, like traction, because I was up and down to sing and the part of me that was down, I was always trying to move around, to maneuver one way or another. I was all there—with my whole heart—but a good part of me never touched that seat. Bill Brown, being a smart gentleman, put a big RESERVED sign on my chair after he sawed the arm off so nobody else with a spill would sit there. They couldn't go sawing off arms all over the place. Oh, boy! I'll never forget that chair. I wish I had it for a trophy.

You'll notice I still haven't said anything about Billy Graham or Cliff Barrows, the musical director, because I hadn't met either of them. That's the funny part. Wild horses couldn't have kept me away from that Crusade because I felt so much love and as though everybody was my friend, but I'd never met most of the main ones. Still, each night Billy would answer something that was on my mind. That precious boy clarified so much for me. That's the word —he clarified. You see, God had prepared me. I was homesick for Jesus. My heart was ready.

During the eighth week, they sent out a petition for you to sign if you were going to stay over, because they *were* planning to extend the meetings. I didn't sign it. I longed to, but I didn't, because there was my house to be sold back in Los Angeles with that freeway coming through and from night to night I didn't know what I was going to do. I had kept my one theater date, and if I was to keep money coming it, I knew I'd better be after more work. But how could I work and attend every one of those meetings? For two months, my life had been as though I was in a long-run play! I knew they didn't need me at the meetings, but how I needed them!

*How I needed to be there!* Except for that one club date, I hadn't missed a night. Being so big kept me tired out, and I knew I should be getting worried about money and work, but all I could think was—one more night. I'll go back to the Garden to hear Billy and be with those Christians *just one more night*.

For sure, I hadn't said a word to anybody but Jesus, and over and over I'd told Him that I wanted to get out of my kind of show business. Then I'd say, *But how? There's no market for what I know how to do other than in my profession. You know that, Lord.*

I didn't hear any voices from heaven, but the first thing I knew I was kind of arguing with the Lord, saying, "I know the type of work I'm doing now in my one-woman shows some would say is all right. That there's no harm to singing 'Am I Blue?' Still, in my heart, Jesus, I'm not so sure about that. I'm not one bit sure! But I don't know how to do anything else to keep myself except sing my kind of song. Oh, I could sing songs about You, but where? Where would the bookings come from? I've got my mother to support along with all the rest of my obligations."

Of course, at the Crusade they knew I had not signed that paper saying that if they extended the meetings, I'd be there. The others around me were signing, signing. I just sat there. Then one night Cliff Barrows took the microphone during choir rehearsal before the service and said over the loudspeakers: "We're going to extend the campaign for four more weeks. And since someone from the audience has requested it, we were wondering if next Tuesday night on television Miss Ethel Waters would sing with the choir, 'His Eye Is on the Sparrow'?"

I was so shocked all I could think was—*what did he say?* And Cliff had to repeat himself. "We've had a request from the audience for Miss Ethel Waters to sing 'His Eye Is on the Sparrow.' Will you come early for rehearsal Tuesday night, Miss Waters, and honor that request with the choir?"

For a second I bowed my head, then I just nodded Yes. They

sent me the paper again and I signed it. I'd stay, and I'd sing "Sparrow." There had been no ballyhoo or buildup. Cliff Barrows had just asked me in that straightforward way and I'd said I would. Knowing I wasn't a churchgoer, knowing I was still in show business, he had asked me to sing. Suddenly, I realized why I hadn't left for Los Angeles. The Lord had other plans for me all the time.

From then till Tuesday night when I was to sing "Sparrow" at the Garden, my old heart pounded even harder than it normally had to pound to get the blood through me. I wasn't scared. I'd sung "Sparrow" before the most critical audiences in the world and won their acclaim, and yet this time, *this* time, I wanted to sing it with more feeling than ever before. I prayed much the same prayer I'd always prayed before a performance: "Lord, help me sing it well. Let me please the people." But even as I said those familiar words, I knew far more was about to happen than for Ethel Waters to please one more audience. And that is why my heart was still pounding as I walked slowly to the microphone that night to sing "Sparrow." Outwardly, I was a distinguished, long-time singing and theatrical star about to repeat one of my most unforgettable songs to thousands of people, in surroundings familiar to me, the old Garden in New York. Inwardly, Ethel Waters knew that something far deeper was taking place.

At last I was about to find out something—for sure.

I sang "Sparrow" that night and I found out.

I found out that the two lives could not mix. I found out right while I stood there singing that I had to make up my mind to continue in the world of the theater with all that meant, or go full time with God. That came just as clearly as it had come to me at age twelve that I could not go back into the little church with hate in my heart. I had never been a fence straddler. For me—understand I'm not speaking for anybody else—but for me, I *knew* one step would lead to another if I went on with my profession. I couldn't do just one thing in the theater. I couldn't earn a living singing "Sparrow" or "Cabin in the Sky" for the rest of my life!

If you're versatile, as I've always been, they're not going to let you pick. I was lucky in *The Member of the Wedding* to get Carson McCullers and the producer to let me change the Russian ditty to "Sparrow," but luck can only be pushed so far. You got to do what they need you to do when you're a performer. It's their money, and when you get a chance at a part, you got to sink or swim—or get off the pot!

I sang "His Eye Is on the Sparrow" for my first time at a Crusade, and standing there was just me and my guilt and Jesus. Jesus had never left me. He had never, not once, turned away from me. I was the one who had turned away from Him. I'd never lost my reverence for God. In fact, like most show people, I had Him on a pedestal. I now know that in what they call the secular world, people have a high, reverent feeling about Jesus Christ—much more than some Christians who take Him for granted.

Standing there singing "Sparrow" that first time at a Crusade, I knew the only thing I had to concern myself with was—forgiveness. Billy Graham had clarified God's forgiveness for me, and as I sang, I received it, and that honesty the dear Catholic sisters had taught me—the kind of almost dogged honesty that had characterized me all my life—paid off again. *I faced up to the fact that I had one big decision to make.*

I would either have to step down from my own pedestal in the world of the theater for which I had worked so hard—or turn my back on God again. I couldn't live both ways at once. Maybe some people can. I knew I couldn't.

I made the decision that night and it wasn't made with any counselor, either. There were no flashbulbs popping when I made it. There were no headlines about it the next day, I was just sitting there, after my song, in my chair with the sawed-off arm, surrounded by all the rest of those choir members. For about a minute, I backed off, but I had looked squarely at what it meant: I had to decide whether Jesus was going to take care of me the rest of my days—whether I was going to live in clover or catnip.

I decided for Jesus, settled down on my now well-seasoned,

armless chair, and listened to Billy in peace—peace of a kind I'd never known before.

Back at the hotel that night I called Floretta Howard at my house in Los Angeles and told her I wasn't coming back home then as I'd planned, and whatever the offer turned out to be on my house, I'd take it.

I stayed until the New York Crusade finally closed and I sang "Sparrow" five times. One day I suggested to Cliff Barrows, who was still pretty much a stranger to me, that if they'd make one of those small records of "Sparrow" with me singing with the New York Crusade choir, I thought they'd get in a lot of money. They did. You see, they believed that when I stood up that first time to sing "Sparrow," I was making my first public witness to my wonderful Saviour. They believed that I was sincere. They took the chance on me, and so far as I know, none of their followers complained. Probably none of the Team had ever seen me in a theater or a movie, had ever heard me sing before that first night, but they let me sing five times, and each time I was more and more convinced that I was at last following God's plan for me.

Don't anybody think I wasn't assailed by doubts. I say that for the benefit of any readers who might be doubting right now as to whether they've done the right or the wrong thing. It isn't easy to give up almost fifty years of something that's tried and true. You worked hard for what you had and you find yourself kinda wishing you could continue on in little bits and spots—but you can't! I've always felt free to do *Member* and you may have seen me sing on other TV shows since then—like the Pearl Bailey show, but you have heard me sing only songs about God and heaven. I had doubts, all right, and not just about how I would make my living, being past sixty and all alone in the world. The Devil tried to get at me with self-doubt too. "You know you got no church voice. You can't do this, Ethel. You can't sing the songs those Christians want." Flip Wilson didn't have his own show then on TV, but I love that boy now and way back then, in 1957, I'd shout like Flip does (and oh, I love that precious boy!), "Devil, you made me do it—you made me doubt! git behind me—git behind me!" He got. Then I'd pray, "Lord, help me. Give me the courage to get up there and do it the only way Ethel Waters knows how to sing. Help me not to worry about *how* I do it. Just let me stay free to do it my own way —help me to just be myself."

The Crusades where Billy preaches are so big and all, it's just not possible for everybody to get acquainted, even on the staff. And although I had worked by that time with Cliff Barrows who led the singing and Tedd Smith, at the piano, I still had only nodded at Billy and knew only a few other Christians by name. They were all warm and wonderful to me and I loved them, but there is one thing some of you who have lived your whole lives inside the Church need to remember. Except for someone who appears on radio and TV like Billy, folks in the world outside just don't know the names of the important people in the Christian world. If you find yourself suddenly a committed Christian as an adult—the way I did—you find yourself just as suddenly in the midst of a world populated by well-known, important, fine, respected people—you know, big shots, leaders—that you've never heard of! You don't mean to be dumb. You don't mean to be superior. You don't mean to be difficult or anything like that, but you just *don't know* those famous people. As I said before, probably no one on the Graham Team was familiar with my show business performances. By the same token, outside of Billy Graham, who'd been preaching to me on radio for years, and that blessed Grady Wilson, who assisted him, and Cliff Barrows and Bev Shea, the Crusade soloist, and Bill Brown, who sawed the arm off my chair, and Lane Adams, who got my first tickets and then my choir button for me—outside of them, I just didn't know *anybody* suddenly. I didn't know hardly anybody even on that New York Crusade. I didn't know the names of Christian organizations or anything like that. None. I'm laughing when I say, in that sense, I'd just come to town!

So, one day before the Crusade closed, during the extended weeks I had been singing "Sparrow" off and on, I received a long-distance call at my hotel from a Mr. George Wilson in Minneapolis. I knew Billy's headquarters were in Minneapolis—I'd heard that on the radio—but I didn't know Mr. George Wilson was a high-up officer in the office there. I had never heard of a movement called Youth for Christ, so *that* was Greek to me. I didn't know Mr. George Wilson was also the president of Youth for Christ. I can still get so tickled when I remember that telephone call, and I thank the Lord that George Wilson knows how to laugh too.

Well, Mr. George Wilson was calling me and he was the president of everything and I didn't know him from Adam's cat and I really ran afoul. You do, you know. You run afoul when you just plain don't know. So, when I got that call from the 13th secretary, who referred me to the 10th secretary, who was calling for the 5th secretary, who switched me to the 3rd secretary, with all those dear young secretaries knowing to bow three times to the East and me knowing nothing, I was getting a little hot under the collar. By then, you don't know who's calling who or who it ends up to be. And I *didn't know* Mr. George Wilson. God knows I wasn't meaning to be disrespectful and George knows now I didn't. You can't be disrespectful to somebody you don't know. There I sat in my suite in the Empire Hotel and finally on the other end of the wire from Minneapolis, Minnesota, came the voice of Mr. George Wilson. "Miss Ethel Waters?" I said I was. "This is George Wilson. I understand you're flying back to Los Angeles when the Crusade closes and we'd like you to stop over en route and sing at Youth for Christ. We'll arrange for your plane reservation."

Loyalty is my middle name and I wasn't about to get involved with anybody else but Billy, who had done so much for me! *This still goes today.* After they saw me on TV from New York with Billy, many people tried to get me to sing for their organizations. I was up for grabs. Oh, boy, they wouldn't have touched me with a ten-foot pole before, but after Billy Graham had given me that

TV exposure—I was THE THING. And you ask if I'm talking about Christians? Yes. Y-E-S. But it was my baby, Billy, who had given me the chance to sing for Jesus. Billy and Cliff, and I wasn't about to do anything *they* didn't know I was doing.

I not only had to get back to Los Angeles because of the sale of my house, I also had some other performances I had to see about canceling now that I was singing for God, and I had to appear on the Tennessee Ernie Ford TV show. I could do that. Ernie would let me sing about Jesus. But, to get back to the subject and the predicate and Mr. George Wilson waiting there on the other end of the line and me totally ignorant of who he was—I said politely, "Well, I don't know. How did you get my number?"

Poor George, of course, got it through the Crusade Team in New York. After all, he runs the headquarters office! But outside of the ones I've mentioned—Billy and Cliff and Grady and so on—my guard was up with anybody else. And *I didn't know Mr. George Wilson* and so—maybe not so politely—I finally said, "No. I can't do it—whatever it is for whatever, I can't do it."

And do you know that George Wilson, who handles most of the business end of the Crusades, had to call Billy long distance and get him to call me and tell me it was all right before I'd stop over and sing at Youth for Christ?

I was still a beginner in all ways. I was just learning to find my way around in the Christian world, and I stumped my toe right off.

The New York Crusade closed and I flew back to Los Angeles, *after* singing at Youth for Christ en route; did the Tennessee Ernie Ford show, and began to try to find out what was going to happen to my house. By then, even though I was fatter than ever and so uncomfortable, finding it harder and harder to get my breath, I was beginning to sense the easing of the burden inside. I'd carried that burden of loneliness for my Lord through so many years, it didn't slide away all at once. But at times, although I faced the loss of my home which I loved, I'd feel so good and so lifted that I'd be almost—a little frightened. I'd be frightened because the tinge of familiarity, the small moments of pure joy, seemed enough like what I once experienced with the Lord after my conversion in the colored church back in Chester, I'd whisper, "Dear Jesus . . . oh, dear Jesus, is this it? *Is this—it?* Am I really back?"

It *was* real and He began to look after me and I needed that. All I had was tied up in that house. I was too fat and too miserable to take any of the offers to play *Member*. I couldn't have held a midget on my lap—it went straight up and down. All fat.

And daily, I found it harder and harder to handle myself. I was ill—too sick to work. I was forced to cancel my West Coast engagements. My Lord knew all that and it wasn't long until I heard from —Mr. George Wilson again. The Crusade people try as hard as they can to follow up on those who become Christians at a Crusade meeting, and as we talked, George told me his brother, Elwood Wilson, and his wife, Donna, and their two boys, Craig and Tod, were in Los Angeles and would drive me or help me when I needed Christian friends. The upshot of it was I asked Wils and his little family to move in to share my home—at least we'd live there together until the freeway knocked it down. They did, and after that house was gone, we went on sharing another for eight years. My doctor had said I absolutely could not live alone, that I was in no condition because of my weight and my heart. So it was the Lord's way of seeing that I had care and a real family in my home with me.

Finally, a cough which had been getting worse and worse brought me to my senses. When Wils and Donna urged me to go to the hospital for what we thought was a deep chest cold, I was not only coughing until I thought I'd black out, everytime I took a breath my chest went *woo-o-o-o-o*. That was when I met my precious doctor, who still looks after me, Dr. Jack Sheinkopf.

He came into my room at the hospital—saw me propped up on those pillows, and he looked first at me, then at Donna and Wils, who were standing right by my bed, and asked, "*Where has she been?* Why hasn't she come for medical help before this?" He could not understand how I could be walking around in that condition! What he didn't know was that I had tickets to leave for another Crusade right then.

You see, after I returned to Los Angeles from the New York Crusade, I missed it all so much, I would call wherever I happened to hear a new Crusade was in progress and ask them if it would be all right if I came. I just wanted to be sure there would be a ticket for me so I could get in and bask in the joy of hearing the music again and listening to Billy preach. He fed my soul and my soul was so hungry. They were kind enough always to let me come, and usually I'd sing a few times too, which made me happier than they will ever know. But Jesus knew.

So there I lay propped in that bed wheezing with Dr. Sheinkopf staring at me. I later learned that he was a musician too and that he'd heard me and loved me down through the years, back when I could still get my breath and was still streamlined. Seeing me in the shape I was in at that time in that hospital bed brought tears to his eyes. He put his arms around me and cradled my big head on his shoulder, saying, "Ethel, you're a sick woman. The fat is covering your heart. I have to be honest with you. I don't know whether it's too late or not."

He didn't try to make it seem easy for me. Agony can't be easy. Agony isn't pretty.

"You might get out of here. You could have a stroke, or—" He hesitated. "I truthfully don't know. I only know you're a sick woman. A very, very sick woman. But I promise you I'm going to do everything I can to help you."

Donna and Wils were wiping their eyes too by then, but I smiled. This is the truth—before God—I really did smile. And that kind, caring, wonderful doctor looked puzzled. "What are you smiling about, Ethel? You must understand me when I say you're a very sick person. *Right now.* You might never leave this hospital under your own power."

I'm telling you the truth. I was still smiling. And I took his hand and I said, "Doctor, I don't expect you to understand, but

I'm going to quote something to you. I know you're familiar with it." And then, very softly, I quoted: "Yea, though I walk through the valley of the shadow of death, I will fear no evil, for *You* are with me."

Jesus had become so real to me by then, even though I knew I might die, I was not afraid. I was *not afraid.*

They kept me in intensive care twenty-three days. I'd have died from the bill if I'd stayed any longer! Thanks to my precious Lord and my precious doctor and my precious friends, especially Donna and Wils who nursed me, I didn't die. I'm still very much here. Over 200 pounds less of me, but I'm here. Still able to travel about due to the selfless and faithful care of my darling children in the Crusade—still able to sing about my wonderful Lord.

One thing I can't do much anymore is hum. Humming makes me cough. Anybody who is around me much knows I still cough and wheeze and carry on sometimes like I'll choke to death, but if you ask me if that ever happens when I'm up there to sing, I can tell you that Jesus keeps it back! I never give it a thought anymore. He just won't let a wheeze come through till we are finished.

Ethel Waters was not pushed into a counseling session, she wasn't dragged down no aisle, she didn't turn to Christ because she was broke *or* a "has been" in her profession. She didn't rededicate her life to Him and to Him only because she knew she was dangerously ill and afraid to die, either.

Ethel Waters knew she was *fat,* but she didn't know her heart was about to be choked off. She came back to Jesus at old Madison Square Garden in New York for one reason—she was homesick. She couldn't stay away from Him any longer.

She fooled dear Dr. Sheinkopf, though, and he's glad. Still glad to this day. And so is Ethel Waters, because, frail and dependent as she sometimes is and no longer young—she's having a ball!

It's wonderful!

# Part Two

I have already said that Billy Graham *clarified* the way home to Jesus for me back in 1957. And once I came home, other things began to be clarified for me too. It was like a big bright light had been turned on and I began to see myself, and even some of the people I had known in the years past, more clearly than ever before. I began to remember things I'd done and brushed aside which needed to be remedied.

I was born in Chester, Pennsylvania, delivered by a Polish midwife in the year 1896. Not 1900 as reported in my previous book, but 1896. If you're reading this book the year it comes out, 1972, I'll be seventy-six years old. If anybody knows that show people lie about their ages, I know it. They do it so they can keep on earning a living. I admit having lied about my age but not for that reason.

I've always hated a lie. Maybe one of the reasons I hate lies is because when I was a child, folks said that if you have a space between your two front teeth like I have, that meant you were a liar. I'm telling the truth. They said that. They believed that.

I was an ornery child, always up to something, tried all kinds of things, and when my second teeth came in, I used to push things to see what I could get between them. In the beginning my front teeth were as close together as anybody's. I made this gap myself! Finally worked till I got a nailhead through there, and as a result

I got many a belt in the mouth because the older people accused me of having a "lie gap." I'd be telling the truth, but they'd be sure I was lying. So, now, come hell or high water, I'm going to tell you the truth, regardless. I might lie for a friend, but by gum swickety, I won't lie for Waters! You've got to take me right straight out the way I am, and if you don't like it—so what!

I've still got those same teeth, by the way, but that space is no "lie gap." I made it with the head of a nail. I hated being trapped into lying about my age—even way back when it all first started that I was born in 1900 instead of 1896. For years this thing has been givin' me fits. And I hope this sets the record straight. I know I was born in 1896 and Jesus knows, just like I know *why* I told that lie in the first place. Oh, you can laugh. I sit here in my apartment in Los Angeles and laugh at myself, but this kind of thing can bug you. Especially when you told the lie in the first place as a favor to a friend! I did.

I lied as a favor to two old friends, Butterbeans and Suzy, and they're both dead now and no help at all in getting me straight with Social Security or any of those people like that. The whole truth of the matter was this: Suzy and Butterbeans and some others wanted to get in on some insurance, but they needed a group of ten. Now, this insurance company wouldn't take just any group of ten people, they wouldn't take anybody that wasn't born until 1900. Well, Butterbeans and Suzy got nine and they begged me—they *begged* me to be the tenth. I gave in, joined up in this insurance thing way back in the thirties. No agent talked me into lying about my age. I didn't do it to appear younger than I was. I did it by getting into this favor thing for friends! You'd think it would have taught me never to do another favor for a friend, but it didn't.

Don't misunderstand. I'm not upset because of *when* I could start drawing Social Security. I accepted that. But it's that lie that bothers me. I want it straight and there are people living right today who knew me then. Why, I was an entertainer in World War I in New York. I was working at a small place called Edmund

Johnson's Cellar billed as "Sweet Mama Stringbean," and I used to entertain the boys when they were comin' and goin' backwards and forwards. Anybody who played there knows my right age. I've worked with Jack Benny. Jack Benny knows how old I am—and he knows it ain't thirty-nine!

The big light that seemed to come on for me when I came home to Jesus also helped me begin to see other people more clearly. People older or younger than me. People of another color. Those who had befriended me grew more precious. We all have prejudices, but seeing better can help us get rid of them. I think we need to see our young people more clearly.

I see no need for a generation gap. You'd be surprised, I know I always am, at the youngsters on both sides—Christian and non-Christian—who love me in spite of my age, which I fervently *hope* has now been established as seventy-six. I don't know what it is that makes them respond to me, but I thank God for it. I've been to so many of the weddings recently. And I've attended because they, the children, invited me. Some even sent for me to come. It must be that these young people love me, because unless they do love me, they wouldn't have me there.

My seventies are being spent almost entirely with younger people. I'm the oldest one on the Crusade Team. But what I want to make clear is that all the young people I've known and still know and who have loved me were not from sheltered, protected Christian homes. I've known and loved all kinds of youngsters and all kinds have loved me. You see, I'm hip. I dig. They've followed me down through the years and let me know of their love. Educated young people in their teens and uneducated, you might say deprived children too—both white and colored. I've had a hand in raising some of them and I've loved them all—good and bad.

And I still say there doesn't need to be a generation gap. I wish I still had some of the hundreds of letters I've received from young people—letters written a long time later—telling me that when they were such and such an age, they used to stand in line to hear me sing or see me in a play and that they just want me to know they still love me. I'm telling you about how much young people love me even *now* when it ain't fashionable anymore to love anybody over thirty, because to me this proves that there doesn't need to be any consciousness on anybody's part of a difference in age *if* we have learned how to communicate with one another. How to *be* with other people no matter their age, so as to keep this barrier down. Back when I played the theaters for so long, these children would come, oh, they'd come in groups and droves and I adored it when they did. They were genuine. What they felt about me was genuine. You know when a young person likes you. When they don't, you know that too. They're just as honest if they don't like you. Both ways they let you know.

Today, I don't agree with plenty that the young people do, and I let them know that and they respect you for letting them know. So, I'm not going all out upholding what some of them do, oh, no. But I do think a lot of their behavior now is because we have not been strong enough with them. We make too much allowance for youth, keep the spotlight on them. We work too hard at trying to please them instead of letting them know we love them enough to warn and discipline. If we took a stand for real values, they'd respect us more. They're *for* simplicity. The kids don't respect us older ones any more, and while some of the blame for this is on their side, a lot is on ours. The children I helped raise respect me to this day. I don't say they do everything I say, they've got their own lives to live, but as far as I'm concerned, they listen and they always did when I spoke. We all need to listen to one another.

Of course, we've got to admit that there are some people—old and young—that are just naturally bad and some just naturally ornery. We need to stop covering up for that! Even if it hits close to home. Even when it shows us adults up for what we really are. That's what it means to me when Jesus said, "When your right hand offends you, cut it off." If it's your child and that child did wrong—admit it. And admit where you failed.

Another thing I see now is that we've treated young people as though they were different from any other people on the face of the earth. We speak and act about them as though they are a village of children set off from the rest of us. That's just not true! The kids won't remain kids forever. They're kids this afternoon and by tonight they're grown up. They're going to be senior citizens tomorrow. They have minds of their own to use, and they don't stay children long. I'm back up to my second childhood, so I know what they're thinking. We can't kid them, and we shouldn't try to kid ourselves about them. We try to kid ourselves about ourselves too, and that won't work either. We have to clean up some corners of our own. We don't like to do that, but the kids sense it. You'd be surprised how young people watch. I know from the way they watch me. I'm talking about Waters now. When I talk to you about how you ought to be with youngsters, I'm talking about Waters too.

I don't see any reason why another thing Jesus said can't apply to our viewpoint about young people today. He said something so true about how easy it is for us to see the speck in our neighbor's eye—or our neighbor's children's eye—or our own children's eye, but can't see the great big beam in our own! One reason I'm living so at peace with the world today is because I know everything that's wrong with Ethel. My constant daily prayer is to thank my precious Saviour for spiritual strength. Satan knows my weak points. He knows 'em! Just like my Saviour knows 'em. What both young and old have got to do is to believe by faith that God is in charge and that He'll overcome. And in order to give God a chance to overcome, we've got to *admit* and by faith believe and receive. We've got to *want* Him.

Another thing my precious Jesus said which applies equally to young and old in relation to each other has to do with turning the other cheek. Sometimes parents won't do this with their children. Sometimes children won't do it with their parents. What I think most of us don't realize is that turning the other cheek doesn't necessarily mean to receive a physical blow on the other side. It means you can be so right and justified in a situation, but when you're attacked for it, just leave it alone. That's obedience to God. To turn the other cheek even when you know you are right. Let Him take the situation in hand. And that isn't easy to do! None of us needs to think we're going to get to the place where this gets easy. Maybe one time we can do it and the next time not. The point is we've all got to keep on—keep, *keep!* Don't let up. I know I haven't learned it yet, but I'm crawlin'. I'm crawlin'. You can get in a rut with Jesus when what He wants is to keep you coming to Him constantly, to teach you something new, something fresh. He wants to keep you *clinging* to Him. Because once you think you're *stapled* to Him, you're no good. He wants to keep us humble before Him. Over and over I have to say, "Where did I go wrong," and cry out, "Lord, what did I do? Show me. Forgive me—because I know I looked away!"

Especially where our children are concerned, we can't look away from Jesus.

Oh, I could turn some of these kids over my knee and it might help them if somebody did just that. But I thank God I've found out that where love is, there does not need to be what they're calling a generation gap.

Before I leave the subject of young people, I just have to remember that darling child George Finola and smile. He's a grown man now, a fine musician and the head of the New Orleans Jazz Museum. But I'll always think of my baby, George Finola, as a young boy because he's loved me since he was a young boy and I've loved him. In his museum he has one of every record I ever made. Since he was a youngster, George has followed me and I just wouldn't take anything for his love. He's seen me in everything I ever did in the theater since he was old enough to go, I guess. Back in the days before the theater became a snake pit, which is what it is now. Back, too, before hi-fi microphones helped make performers without voices into overnight stars. Back when a voice had to be a voice! I just never knew, and still don't, when George

Finola might turn up. I guess George had written me a lot of letters, but we'd never met until several years ago, in Chicago, one night after a Crusade where I'd sung.

Anybody that knows me or has seen me on TV knows that I don't walk well anymore. If I can know somebody's arm is there, or if I'm in my own apartment, where I can touch a piece of furniture along the way, I get along. But out in a crowd, like after a Crusade meeting, someone leads me in and out wherever I'm heading. So, one night in Chicago, I was trying to get through the crowd and across the street to the car that would take me to my hotel. They had cops to help me too, but this time they had new cops who didn't know my problem in walking. Well, a young fellow was standing there, waiting. It was George. George got me in a wheel chair and pushed me across like I was some kind of queen! I didn't know who he was, but I thanked him and blessed him and just loved him dearly for his kindness. I really did. I just loved that boy right off. And I've loved him from that moment on. To this day, we don't have a generation gap between us!

And just two years ago, when I again played Berenice Sadie Brown for a six-week run in *The Member of the Wedding* at the Ivanhoe Theater in Chicago, precious George Finola was there— not once, but *ten times!* He came and brought his mother and father. His father's a dentist and the whole family is beautiful. And this is a kid who knows my age because he has done more research on me from my records than anybody else. So, when this thing came out about me being born in 1900, very sweetly my baby, George, sent me a long list of my recordings and at the top he had written, "Born in 1896." I thought it was the cutest thing!

I knew George Finola by correspondence before I came all the way home to Jesus, but I love him even more now, because in this "light" I see him more clearly.

During that same 1970 run of *Member* in Chicago, another friend I'd known for years came to see the play, too, and although I doubt I was able to let her know, I felt more devotion and appreciation for her than ever before. Her name is Mrs. Ashton Stevens, the widow of one of the country's most prominent critics, who gave me my first hand up in the world of white theater. I had loved Mr. and Mrs. Ashton Stevens years before, but my feelings were free to run still deeper now.

Back in the twenties, when I was still on the colored circuit working with TOBA (Theater Owners Booking Association), my beloved friend and accompanist, Pearl Wright, and I were booked to do a show at the Grand Theater in Chicago. At the theater that night, because I was with TOBA and not in one of those big productions like *Plantation Days,* there wasn't no dressing room for Ethel Waters! When I remember it, Lord have mercy, I've got to stop and laugh. But I'm telling you the truth about the way it is among us colored, or the way it can be. (Still laughing!) On that one big show, everybody was supposed to be starring. You know, from this show, from that night club—but *that* night on that all-colored revue, Pearl Wright and I had to dress underneath the stairs in the basement—behind a sheet hung up for us. We came new to the show and that was our dressing room.

The show ran long—I mean, they had the *top* colored talent. And you know, we've got the talent. It was all dynamite! In those days which are gone forever, though, there was a friendly challenge of abilities in show business. It's pitiful now. Today, it's a combat to the death. But then, it was a healthy rivalry. Everybody got out there—the whole white downtown had paid their money—and they got a show. I knew my followers from the stockyards were way up in the gallery. Smells and foot stompin' and all, I knew *my* fans were in the gallery. The Nordics (I used to distinguish that way—and I'm laughing!) were in the expensive seats downstairs, but the "natives" were in the gallery.

Well, all evening long these great acts, they would come on. And I mean, they would *come on.* And at twenty-five minutes to eleven o'clock, yours truly walked out there. Everybody had been on but Waters. They looked around to make sure of that, and just before calling the janitor on stage, they said it was all right for me to go on. Oh, boy, I walked out there and I could have cleaned up for the janitor, because I'm telling you, I rocked the Grand Theater and everybody in it. My friends from the stockyards appeared to have left their stink behind, but brought their applause along. Waters wasn't about to let them down!

The next day I noticed the other members of the revue running to the street to buy the latest edition of the paper. I didn't buy it and I couldn't figure why they were so excited. Even when they kept telling me with bated breath that *Mr. Ashton Stevens* had been there that night, I still couldn't figure why all the fuss. They were hunting for his review of our show, but I didn't know Mr. Ashton Stevens and didn't care to know him. I was happy with my boys from the stockyards, stompin', whistlin' and clappin' their hands—for *me*. But then when the big Sunday paper came out, they all just about went crazy. When they looked for the review of our show, there it was—the first time in history, they told me, that Mr. Ashton Stevens had ever run a headline like this:

ASHTON STEVENS FINDS YVETTE GUILBERT OF
HER RACE IN ETHEL WATERS!

The review went on to say, "A new star discovered on State Street, Ethel Waters is the greatest artist of her race and generation." I later learned that this beautiful review had been picked up by newspapers all over the country and people were comparing me with Raquel Miller and Eleanor Duse. I was just flabbergasted and stood blinking at the others in the cast—the big colored stars from gazunk and gazink—they tried to be polite about it, but I knew they were all ready to lynch me! You know, we can all be cannibals now and then, when the occasion is right. But so help me, I didn't even know who Mr. Ashton Stevens was! I kept asking, Who *is* he? What does he do?

The next week people wrote in to thank Mr. Stevens for reviewing me the way he did, as though he had been courageous to headline a Negro, and, did it make him angry! He said he was not apologizing for what he had written because he considered me an *artist*. So, that laid to rest all those people who thought he was just being nice for giving me, an unknown colored girl, that break. He went on to say that it was all a good show, but Ethel Waters blacked out everything else.

That was the beginning of a sincere and beautiful and lasting friendship between me and Ashton Stevens and his lovely wife. And so in 1970, when I was doing *Member* in Chicago at the Ivanhoe, Mrs. Ashton Stevens came out to see her *friend,* Miss Ethel Waters. There was no race gap.

There really is none, but it took me a long time to learn that. What the Lord used further to break down my own prejudice against whites was coming to know one of the kindest, most intelligent and talented gentlemen who ever lived in this world, Carl Van Vechten, a wonderful writer, critic, and the man who took the best photographs of me in the old days. Carl saw so much beyond what most people saw about me as a human being. He liked me for myself. I must admit I didn't trust him, didn't believe that at first. And I'm changing on this score, I'm still learning. My wonderful Lord has had to be, still has to be, very patient with me.

I was never a person to try to kid you or try to put my best foot forward in order to impress you. If you had it, I figured, you'd see it in me, and that went double. If you had it, I'd see it in you. But if you didn't have it, you wouldn't see it in me—so forget it. That was before I really turned all the way to the Lord, you see. In those days, I figured that nobody's going to give you credit for virtues that *they* don't possess. If they ain't got it, they ain't going to credit you with it, so there's no use breaking your brains up to prove nothing. In a way, I'm still like that. Just not so mean about it. This may sound crazy, but I'm talking sense. Might be pig latin to somebody else, but it's still my kind of sense. I always tried to be myself and I still do and I don't find fault with anybody who can't understand me or doesn't like me. I now know that if a person

Miss Waters as a young actress. *Murray Korman.*

As Miss Calico in *Africana* in 1927. *Jay Mitchell*

Singing "Hottentot Potentate" in *At Hom Abroad* in 1935. *Richard H. Tucker*

Miss Waters "On Stage!" *Candid Illustrators*

The famous "Stormy Weather" sequence photographed by Carl Van Vechten, 1933.

Miss Waters with
Archie Savage and
Dooley Wilson
in *Cabin in the Sky.*

*Lew Leslie's Blackbirds,* 1930, included an imitation of Rudy Vallee, with Eubie Blake as accompanist. *White Studio*

A joyful moment is shared with Julie Harris on the opening night of *The Member of the Wedding*, 1950. *Ruth Orkin*

With Carson McCullers and Julie Harris at the opening night party at producer Robert Whitehead's apartment. *Ruth Orkin*

Miss Waters in the 1930's. *Carl Van Vechten*

doesn't like me, that's no reason why I have to dislike him. God's taught me a lot about this point. His light shines bright here. He's taught me to humble myself even when it costs me. But back then I'd try at least to find out why somebody disliked me. I didn't go around begging them to like me, but at least I wondered. Truth is, I really expect I froze in those days if I wasn't liked. At least inside. And I'm not thinking only of difference in color here. I'm thinking about people as a whole. I'm digging into *people*—me included. You see, most of my family didn't like me and I never understood why. They just never, never understood me. I was nothing like Louise Howard who borned me. I was probably something they feared because they couldn't understand me. My grandmother loved me because she understood me—Sally Anderson. But not the rest of my family. I scared 'em, I guess. In the slums people thought I was a terror. I was. I stood out like a sore thumb. Now, I'm not talking about the loyal public that have liked me for my artistry— I'm just talking about me as a private person.

But Carl Van Vechten, that good and sensitive man, understood me almost the first minute we met, and he didn't have much reason to, either. I certainly didn't try to get him to. In those days they all used to say I was a rebel. I was and more than that, I was a person who had a way of speaking my mind too quickly—lots of times just to let off steam. Just to hear myself talk. You know how some people like to open their mouths and say Yah-ya-ya. Well, I was that way. I had built a wall around myself to cover all the hurt and loneliness . . . I said I didn't like a certain thing, but it was because I couldn't have it. I'd say I didn't want that certain thing, because I knew I couldn't afford it. So that I built up a thick wall around me and, children, it can envelop and shut you off so that nobody can help you and when you cry, you cry alone. You cry, you blow your nose and dry your eyes, and then you come right out with another smart, show-off remark, so nobody knows how hurt you are. Nobody knew then if I'd been cut and hurt, because I'd come back at you with such a rapierlike thrust that I could always top

Miss Waters in the final scene from "The Member of the Wedding."

you! I was always in control, believing an eye for an eye and a
tooth for a tooth. People didn't get too close to me. I stayed on
the defensive. I was just always full of hurt and hiding it.

Well, not too long after Ashton Stevens gave me that rave review and before he and Mrs. Stevens and I became close friends, I
was back in New York working at the Lafayette. The Lafayette
was the *crème de la crème*—only the high echelon in the colored
theater played it. The Lincoln on 135th Street was the colored
variety house. All the white people used to come there to catch the
entire colored vaudeville, and then they'd go to the Lafayette
where the really terrific colored *drama* went on. All the big names
worked at the Lafayette and believe me, we had some beautiful
colored actresses and actors and it was strictly legit, not vaudeville.
The Lincoln belonged to B. F. Keith, and the only way my race
could attend was to sit in the gallery. Not just the balcony, but the
*gallery*. That wasn't unusual, you know. They did that in the
South too. And honestly, the colored did—at least a certain kind—
make a whole lot of noise. Some colored, light enough to pass, sat
downstairs with the whites and nobody knew. In those days, all
colored didn't really want to be colored! Didn't want to be "black
and beautiful"—they just wanted to enjoy the show. Oh, Lord,
have mercy, I'm laughing about all of us—white and colored and
in-between. Anyway, white agents would come up there and book
these talented big names in the colored theater world, sandwich
them in with the B. F. Keith acts, and take them around.

Well, Carl Van Vechten was always coming to the theater then,
gathering material for his book, *Nigger Heaven*. When he put that
book out, he had all the ultra-ultra of the colored society at his
home often. They were welcome, really welcome guests. Carl was
cosmopolitan. To his house also would come the biggest names in
the white world of the theater and publishing. Carl knew them all
and they all knew him. All but me, that is. I didn't want to know
him!

All this, of course, was way back when I was in my twenties, although I'd been traveling in vaudeville for a long time and had met with that big success in Chicago. When *Nigger Heaven,* a novel about Harlem, first came out, I was the one that pitched the riot act. I didn't know Carl Van Vechten from Adam's house cat and cared less and proceeded to blow my mouth and talk my big talk when I hadn't read his book and wasn't going to read it. I tell you, I carried on like a yard dog! People would say, "But, Ethel, you're *in* the book." And I'd tell them, "Well, I don't want to be in it!" You see how contradictory we are? All of us, and that means me too. Me especially then. I'm here to tell you that plenty of us aren't ready yet, and for sure, I wasn't ready then.

So, one day not long after Carl's book came out, I was over at the Lafayette doing a run with one of Lew Leslie's shows and here comes a card back to my dressing room: "Dear Miss Waters, will you please give audience to Mr. Carl Van Vechten?"

And with the loudest, bawdiest voice, I yelled, "Why? Is this supposed to be nigger heaven? I thought it was the Lafayette!"

Do you know, that dear, lovely man ignored me, came right on up the stairs and into the room where I was making all that noise? I can still see this pleasant, wonderful gentleman standing there, smiling at feisty Ethel. He had a delicious sense of humor and he stood there laughing in his kind way and said, "Hello, how are you?" Before I knew it, I was laughing too, and we sat down and talked and laughed some more together, and there was just something about him that made me realize how wrong I had been.

I had spouted off against the man and I didn't even know him. Had never, until that minute, laid eyes on him. On his side, there had been no prejudice. It was all on mine because we didn't know each other before.

From that time on and all down through the years until he died, we had this sincere and wonderful friendship. My precious baby, Carl, his wife, Fania, and I. More than once—many times—he'd give splendid affairs at his home with so many famous people it would make your head swim. And Carl would invite them to come this way: "I want you to meet Miss Ethel Waters." I was neither a VIP, nor was I on Skid Row. I was—Ethel Waters, the young woman this fine, greathearted man wanted them all to know.

Later on, when I starred on Broadway in *Mamba's Daughters,* I really knew that I had made some genuine friends at Carl and Fania's house, because Dorothy Gish, Oscar Hammerstein, Judith Anderson, Burgess Meredith, John Emery, and Tallulah Bankhead, along with Carl, himself, placed an ad they paid for out of their own pockets—in *The New York Times,* urging the public to see "Ethel Waters' superb performance . . . a profound experience" in *Mamba's Daughters* on Broadway.

Carl was my first dear white friend.

I see very clearly now that Carl understood me. *Me.* He didn't expect me to fit into his mold. He was very positive in his thinking and very sensitive. He didn't miss anything. I refreshed him, he used to tell me, because he was so sick of so many folks always trying to be somebody else, you know, like that. Trying to be what they weren't. Here's a time that illustrates what I mean by this. One night he gave a big dinner. Now, I'm very honest and blunt about things and I don't and didn't mean to be stupid. If I'm stupid, I'm not apologizing for it, because one person can't know everything.

It's been more than forty years ago that I went this particular night for the first time to Carl's fine, gorgeous apartment. He had a butler and elegant furniture and art pieces and everybody was there, with this one and that one—all bowing to this side and that side.

Anyway, that night, the first course they served was borsch. I looked at mine. I looked at Carl. I looked back at the borsch and I said, "Huh-uh. Not me." Carl laughed and said, "Oh, but it's delicious!" And again I said, "Not for me." Then I asked, "What is it?" And Carl said, "Why, it's cold beets and—well, you tell me, Ethel, what does it look like?" And I said, "Well, it looks like it's just beet soup and clabber and I don't like either one!"

I didn't eat it, because I *don't* like clabber and I don't like cold

beet soup, and the fact that he said it was Russian didn't get to me
at all. Next came this other select dish—caviar. Fish eggs. I shook
my head again. "Huh-uh. Looks like buckshot and Carl, there ain't
no use pretending. I like scrapple, but I don't like cold beets and
clabber and I don't like fish eggs."

I wasn't saying all that to be Uncle Tom or Aunt Tomasina,
either one. I was telling the truth, I just plain love scrapple. Carl
was from Pennsylvania too. He knew what scrapple was. I was
just being me and Carl accepted me and understood me that way,
so much beyond what my own family did.

Carl was talking to some of those famous people one day and
he said, "You know, it's a funny thing about Ethel. She never asks
for anything and she never thanks you for anything." Come to
think about it, I don't think I ever did either one much. I try to
remember to say please and thank you, and I know that I do now
since Jesus, but then, I didn't really know what Carl meant.
Especially when he said I didn't ask for anything. Now I think I
see he was double-talking. I think he meant I never played up to
anybody seeking favors. And I still don't. Not by the merest
whisper. Some of my children, lots of them, are the top names in
the business today, and if I were to give the barest hint, they'd
come to my rescue for anything I needed. Why, there'd be a standing line! But I find that I can't even express publicly how much and
how often I think of them—some at least—without them getting
the wrong impression. And the reason for this is that "asking" has
been abused so much. Abused by both colored and white. But
Carl Van Vechten thought of me and understood me as just another
human being whom he liked and whose talents he recognized. It
had nothing to do with me asking or with me being colored and
him white.

If we stop to think about it, we're all colored.

I'm one color and you may be another. And when I say there's
no difference under the skin, I mean mainly that we're all sinners
in need of a Saviour. The same Saviour who loves us all alike.

I've been a person who respected myself for what I was. I've always thought you earned respect. So much of the talk nowadays is about "What *we* have coming to us" instead of understanding a whole lot of things that I was raised with and stuck with. Like they bellyache now about doing hard work and honest labor. Both colored and white. That to me was no problem. I didn't object to it when I was young and I wouldn't now. Hard work wasn't something to riot about or march against or apologize for back in my day. My grandmother was a hardworking woman and kind to all people. She couldn't do anything but honest labor—nothing but cook, wash, iron, and scrub. Nowadays, nobody wants to do that. I don't understand this! I don't say you shouldn't try to better your station, but don't downgrade people that can't do anything else and don't poke fun at them that are satisfied with their lot.

I never was a leader and nobody could lead me and I never was a follower and I didn't follow nobody. I'm my own individual. I always was. I admit when I was young I did not like white people. Only my dear Lord knows how grateful I am for releasing me from my childhood prejudices which would have blocked me from listening to Billy Graham!

# Part Three

It's true no one ever wants to stay a loner. But when you've been one as long as I have, it seems as though you'll never get used to the fact that at long last, you're surrounded by people who really love you for yourself. Not because you've been a success, but because you're *you*. I want to tell about some of these children with whom I live and work now and I will have to begin with that kind Dr. Billy Graham. What I'll have to say is going to surprise a lot of people too, because even though I love that boy with all my heart and owe him more than he will ever understand, I really don't know Billy Graham very well. People think I do. So many people ask me all about him, like I'm one of his closest friends.

Well, let me tell you something. A man in Billy's position can't have many close friends. I don't know of anyone on the Crusade staff that doesn't love and respect him, but he lives his life so much in the limelight, with so many demands on his time and with people's ears open to every word he lets drop (sometimes so they can twist it all around), he just can't live a normal life. I suppose there's as many different opinions of the boy as there are people pulling at him, trying to get at him for this or that. And brother, he's criticized too. I know!

No man and no woman ever rises as high as Billy has without having rocks thrown at his head. He expects that, but I see enough about him to know Billy's human and he has to cling to God minute by minute in order to keep immune from both the rocks and the bouquets!

I've already told you that for me, at first, his good looks got in the way. I know this is true with others besides me. Billy can't help that. He's just as natural and quiet and gentle as a man can be. He's reserved. He's had to be. If he weren't, people would tear him to pieces. He's never told me this, but I know he's had to learn how to walk that narrow line between being aloof and reserved. Billy's not arrogant. He doesn't have an arrogant bone in his big tall body! He has natural dignity, and except for a few members of the Team, he doesn't dare permit himself close friends, but he's always nice and pleasant.

This may also surprise you, but I've never been to the Graham home. There isn't any explanation or reason for this. I've been to the homes of other members of the Crusade Team, but this is a busy, busy man and when he has a chance to be at his home with his lovely wife, Ruthie, who can blame him if they don't fill the house with people? He needs that rest. He really needs it. So the only time I see Billy Graham is at the Crusades or when I'm asked to go along and sing like when he receives an award or something. I'm honored and I always go. I'll always go if Billy wants me or needs me as long as I can slip one foot past the other! After that, they can push me in a wheel chair. But I see my child mainly at the Crusades. Still, people tend to think we're kissin' cousins. We're not. He is always considerate, as are all the others on the Team, and they know that my first loyalty is to Billy. My first loyalty is to Billy and it will always be. I owe every priority to Billy Graham, and although I go when any of the Associate evangelists call for me if I possibly can make it with my physical limitations, Billy will always be first with me because Jesus brought me back to Himself through Billy's preaching. He feeds me now through Billy, along with the others who preach the Word of God. I still search the radio dial for a Crusade broadcast when I'm alone lots of times. I might be here or there or right in my own apartment, but everytime I hear the Graham theme and hear the words "This is the Hour of Decision," I say, "Oh, thank You, Jesus, I'm going to get to hear Billy preach about You!"

I never would have been exposed to the Christian life and the Christian world as I know it now without Billy. Columbus discovered America, but Billy Graham helped me express my love for Jesus Christ by allowing me to sing "Sparrow" back in 1957 at Madison Square Garden. All else lovely came after that. But that was number one. I know Billy and everybody connected with that New York Crusade was on the spot when they asked me—a woman still in show business weighing 350 pounds—to sing on TV. Only God my father wasn't on the spot. Billy and Cliff Barrows took a chance. I wasn't even a church woman! I believed, but I was still in the theater, yet those darling men let me sing and the people believed me. *They believed me.* After that, everything was okay, but who took the risk? Billy Graham and Cliff Barrows and whoever else had a say. Since that night when I first sang "Sparrow" with Billy, I've tried every minute to give praise to my wonderful Saviour for all these unspeakable blessings.

Of course, since Billy took that chance, I get into some tight places now and then when other big evangelists call and beg me to sing with them. I make it plain (and I can still do that!) that I refuse to clash with anything Billy Graham does. I owe that to Billy. I'm not going on any television program or any platform that's going to crowd Billy!

Billy Graham is my raven. I've got others now, but God sent Billy first to feed me. Still, in spite of how deeply I love and respect Billy Graham, I never pressure my friendship on him. Why, the whole time I was attending that first Crusade in New York, I'd only see him from where I sat, and even after I sang, he'd shake hands with me and say something like "God bless you." I have to laugh now remembering this, but then I just about idol-worshiped all the Team, and once, *once* in a room downstairs at the Garden, I ran into Billy and I was so glad and so happy to see him up close, I squeezed that boy until I almost crushed a rib! I know I must have hurt him, because the next time I saw his wife, Ruth, she said, "Don't give me the kind of hug you gave my husband or I'll break in two!"

To this day, I just can't stress too much that my joy is to sit and be fed by that boy. I'll never forget when the Crusade came to San Francisco and I called to see if they'd let me attend. I was just full of joy! In the beginning I would always ask them if I could come. I'd never go without asking first. You see, I didn't want to force myself on them. Not ever. But they'd give me permission no matter where the Crusade was. People don't know that. I don't know what they think happened, but they don't know I was just that eager to be fed from the Word of God by Billy. Back in the beginning and for several years, people would say, "Ethel, Billy likes you." I don't know what it was that made him like me, but I thank my precious Jesus that he did and does. I know Billy's children and Ruth like me too, and that gives me more joy.

I've learned so much about really being loved from the wives of the Associate evangelists and the musicians. These wives are the unsung, unheralded evangelists! It's the *wives* of these dedicated men that keep the husbands on the firing line. They carry the burden and I know what I'm talking about. It's the women who keep the families together, and it can only be God who keeps their loneliness back. They have to meet domestic problems for both husband and wife so much of the time, and only God keeps them steady. Ruthie Graham and Billie Barrows and Irma Shea, Bev's wife, and Wilma Wilson, Grady's wife, and the others—what a job they all do in holding back their loneliness for their husbands and managing their homes alone. And they love their men. They love them dearly. I know for a fact, just because the men have been gone so much of the time for so many years, that their loneliness and missing does not grow less.

Why, I have seen Cliff Barrows come in from a rehearsal many times on a Crusade, so dog tired—his eyelids only half open—but never too tired to call his lovely, adorable wife, Billie. And his poor tired face will just light up at the sound of her voice because he'd been so hungry for her words. He needed to hear it straight from Billie that things were all right. That she was all right. People don't think I would observe these things, but I do. The wives on the other end of those telephone calls have to let their husbands feel that it's all—all right. I couldn't prove that, but somehow I know it. I sense it. I learn about being loved from them.

And how I have learned about love from that precious child, Ruth Graham! What a woman, what a woman, *what a woman*. I'll never, never forget one night when I was with the Crusade in London at Earl's Court. Ruth was there too for this one. It was a huge place and I had to leave a little early, on account of walking so poorly and so slowly and having to touch a wall or something when I go along in order to keep my balance. Well, I was trying to get outside before the crowd left and that's when I saw Ruth, making her way down the stairs, holding onto a drugged teen-aged girl. Now, I *saw* this. And there was no photographer to take her picture to make her look good and there was no newsman to write her up. Nobody was there except that understanding, loving Ruthie Graham alone, trying to hold onto this kid who was so drugged her eyes were rolling. She was really on a trip. An overdose. And delicate-looking little Ruth wasn't gingerly touching this girl, who was almost twice her size. Ruth Graham was enveloping her in her arms—embracing her, almost carrying her to her own car to take her safely away from the crowd. Out of the corner of my eye, as I stood there near that wall, I saw two people supposed to be like guards, ushers or whatever they called 'em, who *could* have come out and assisted Ruth. Do you think they moved? They looked the other way. Maybe because that girl, poor child, wasn't what you'd call clean, she was a dirty hippie type. But there was Ruth, embracing her, *showing* her the love of God. The girl had come to Billy's meeting somehow and Ruth cared enough to give her time and herself just to that one stoned kid out of all the crowd. If Ruth Graham had been wearing a fashionable fur coat, there would have been someone there at least to remark, "How can she afford a fur coat married to an evangelist?" No one was there watching *this* but me. Nobody was helping that precious woman at all. Ruth saw me and stopped at the foot of the stairs with the girl and said to her, "I want you to meet Miss Ethel Waters." Ruthie called the child's name, but I've forgotten what it was. The girl tried to come to enough to say something. I could see her struggle to focus her eyes, like maybe she was trying to acknowledge my name.

But the thing I noticed most was the way Ruth held her in her arms and didn't once let her go.

The wives of these men are great women. I love them and I thank God that they seem to love me. Ruth Graham, Wilma Wilson, Billie Barrows, Irma Shea, Thelma Smith, Don Hustad's wife, Ruth, lovely Helen Wilson, George's wife, Winola Wirt, Dr. Sherwood Wirt's wife (I call her Twinkletoes), Jean Ford, Leighton's wife—they're all beautiful women. All marvelous, great women. They sacrifice normal family life—they love their husbands, they dearly love them, but they sacrifice companionship to stay with the children, to make good homes, because they know the children need them.

I'm a loner. I've always been, but these things I know and I know from being with them. Who gave them that sacrificial strength? Jesus. Jesus. They've got to have His strength to get past the time when maybe they don't hear from their husbands when they hoped to due to travel mixups and so on. They've got to have strength to keep down worry and human complaints, to keep down their own longings and loneliness.

Sometimes Ruthie will just call me up for no reason, just to talk, or I'll write her a little note—"Hi, precious . . ." or I'll get her number and call her to say Hello and tell her I love her. That I'm thinking about her. It's uncanny, people really are *one* in Jesus. The old saying is right—"It takes one to know one." Jesus is in the hearts of these women and the same Jesus is in my heart. He keeps us close and loving each other even though we can't be together much in this hurrying world.

So many times, sitting in my apartment by the big window, just thinking about my new family the Lord has supplied, my thoughts go back to that first Crusade in New York when, out of my loneliness, I came back to Jesus. In the brightness of His light now, I can see how many barriers have fallen down in me since those days when I first met some of the people on the Team then. I think how I idolized them. The years of working with them have showed me how to love them and trust them as human beings. I recall the first ones who had been with Billy from the beginning . . . my precious, good-humored Grady Wilson, his brother, T. W. Wilson, Bev Shea with his beautiful voice, Lane Adams, Howard Jones, Bill Brown, Fred Dienert, Willis Haymaker, Walter Bennett, Akbar Haqq, and of course, my child, Tedd Smith, who still plays for me so often.

I think of the ones in recent years who have become prominent, like Leighton Ford and his fine choir director, Irv Chambers. Leighton usually has me come with him for two days, and always, during our time together, he drops in once or twice a day and has prayer with me. A very sweet, attentive boy and I love him. Intelligent. Dedicated.

I have to say that I feel especially close to Grady Wilson and his dear wife, Wilma. There are probably three reasons for this, and one of them is that I've sung so often with Grady on his Crusades. Some of the Associate Evangelist Crusades aren't exactly as posh as people may think, either. We stay where we can and Grady or one of the others will preach and I'll sing—sometimes out in the middle of a field somewhere. I really like those better in many ways, because the people in the smaller places are often so warm and full of love. The second reason I am so close to the Grady Wilsons is that it just seems like Grady and Wilma are always there when I need them. To me, Grady and Wilma are in a photo finish with Billy and Ruth. But the circumstances of the meetings and our travel and so on have just made it come out so that I've been in Grady's home so often and in his car with him driving here or there or with that loving Wilma taking me backwards and forwards to where I need to go in the way that makes it always easiest for me, though not for her.

Knowing Grady so well, I take a lot of joy too in being so sure that Grady Wilson *really loves Billy Graham*. He and his brother T. W. look out for Billy, the human being. When he's traveling, Billy will call Grady in the middle of the night sometimes to come and be with him. In a way, Billy's a child and I know, oh, how I know he gets lonely just for down-to-earth companionship. Grady goes out of his way to bear the brunt for Billy. He gets hurt for him. He'd die for him. He would. Grady Wilson would die for Billy, his friend. So, the second reason I feel so close to Grady is because *I know him*. He's very outgoing. Everyone loves him. But his disposition is real. He's not a phony. He's real and he's a man! A good man, Grady Wilson is.

The third reason I feel so close to Grady is because he has a terrific sense of humor. Why, he and I can always find a good belly laugh to ease things up, especially on some of our smaller Crusades.

Of course, Grady and I can laugh (and we do!) at what could sometimes be the wrong places. But it usually turns out all right because my precious Lord has a sense of humor too. How do you think we got ours? Not from the Devil. No, sir. He don't have any!

I'll tell you about one night in particular I'll never forget and I never mention it without having to stop and laugh all over again. This didn't happen on one of Grady's Crusades when we were out there working together, either. This happened at one of the big ones, in Pittsburgh, when I was singing with Billy. This will just show you how ornery my baby, Grady Wilson, really is. How ornery and how lovable. I'm sitting there on the platform waiting till it's my turn to sing. Because it looked as though there was going to be a terrible storm, we were all tense. The time came for me to get up and give my witness before I sang, and when anybody gets up to do his thing in a Crusade, generally the person closest will say, "Holding you in prayer." They do, and this is sincere. It really is. So, just as I was getting ready to get up, Grady passed me and said very softly, "Your slip is showing!"

Well, I let out a big whoop right there in front of those thousands of people, and even though I knew they were all staring at me, puzzled, I still couldn't stop laughing. But I managed to get to the stand where I was to sing, and there still sat all those people staring at me, wondering what to do next and me still laughing so hard I almost couldn't talk.

Finally, I said, "I might just as well tell you people what happened. Grady just passed me and instead of saying he was holding me in prayer as I expected, he told me my slip was showing!"

I mean to say that stadium rocked. The people howled! They laughed so hard it broke the tension wide open! There wasn't no more tension around *anywhere* after that. Now, God did that. You can't tell me He didn't. We all needed to be loosened up and He loosened us through my ornery baby Grady's knocked-out teasing.

Oh, I've got the stories about Grady on our Crusades. The Lord looks after Grady and me every minute. He has to, because, although we both love Him (and how Grady does love Jesus!) we *are* both ornery.

One time coming out of Biloxi, Mississippi, after a Crusade, Grady took me and his daughter, Connie, who was with us, to an out-of-the-way spot famous for its food. Connie had been sleeping in the back seat of the car, so told her daddy and me to go on inside while she fixed her hair. On the way in I said, "Grady, you know where we are, don't you?" I meant Mississippi, but Grady never gives such things a thought, so in we marched. Two women ran the restaurant (glad I can't recall their names) and both of them looked at Grady, then at me. The double take was unanimous! He politely pulled out my chair and ordered our steaks. I could tell a few customers recognized me, but while they were my fans, they didn't know this white fellow with me and you know what they were thinking!

In a minute or so in came Connie and that really mixed them up. Eventually the steaks came—mine the smallest of the lot— and literally thrown down in front of me by the waitress. After awhile somebody told the two women who owned the place who I was. They were genuinely embarrassed, but I could tell they still couldn't forgive me for coming inside in the first place, let alone with a white man.

And Grady's wife, Wilma? Besides being able to keep up with Grady's humor, Wilma Wilson is one of the darlingest women on earth. And here again, I know this to be true. Wilma is a saint. She knows Jesus. Why, often Grady has to substitute for T. W., looking after Billy, say when T. W. has to be home with his family. Lots of times I've known this to happen when Grady has just come off a Crusade and is so tired and so longing to be at home a day or so with Wilma and the children. Wilma, you can be sure, is longing to have him home, but she's never said a word when Grady has to go right off to be with Billy. Billy needs him, Billy is God's front man, and off Grady goes. To be with Billy, to protect him from some of the pressures that surround him. Pressures under the guise of Christianity.

Loving Billy as I do, I'm glad Grady's the one who can always crash that private door. There are only a few men who really look after Billy and Grady's one of 'em. And Wilma is glad, because she loves Billy too. I can tell by a person's Hello whether they're sincere or not. I've been burnt so often and a burnt child dreads fire, but Billy is so trusting and good and so busy, he *needs* protection. There are *pressures* from some folks who call themselves God's people, but I'll tell them straight to their teeth that they can't be. My dear Jesus said that you can't serve God and mammon. So you decide. Some people, and they may really respect Billy sincerely, hover around him for commercial reasons and he's got too much on his mind to have to handle this kind of thing.

But to get back to my baby, Wilma Wilson. Like I've already said, some of the big Crusades are done up in style, really nice. But sometimes with Grady and me—oh, boy, you talk about barnstorming! Yet when Wilma's along to help us, as she is when she possibly can make it, none of the ruggedness and heavy driving and bad weather bothers her. And always, she's seeing to it that her husband, Grady, has peace of mind. I was with them about two years ago, when Wilma drove over 125 miles a day—backwards and forwards from a Crusade—to the hospital when Grady's Dad was so low—just so Grady would have the latest report.

Wilma and I have had some laughs too. She and Grady know all the great restaurants and there was one she wanted me to try. On the way in I said, "Wilma, this is North Carolina." She said, "Oh, Ethel, you mustn't think like that!" The place served family style and was very crowded that day. When I walked in, lots of people recognized me and smiled warmly. Not the owner. She looked Wilma over, then me, as if to say, "Well, I guess she's with her Madam."

When our food came, mine was put on the table *next* to us, so that Wilma had to reach over and get it, at which point I said, "Wilma, I told you to bring my apron!" Well, we just about broke up laughing. But before we finished our meal, a relief girl came on duty, who took one look at me and gasped, "Oh, Miss Waters!" You should have seen that owner's face. It blanched. I think she even managed to mutter, as we left, "Do come back."

Another time I remember I had just come in from Canada, riding all night, and I was nearly dead when I got to Wilma's, and that darling girl had to drive all around town to get me one of those portable oxygen things. Time after time she has driven me —through all kinds of weather—I don't know how many miles to an airport to catch a plane to get me wherever it was I had to go. Once, I remember when she had come a long way to get me from a Crusade, and took me back to her house to rest. But Wilma didn't rest—she just stretched across the foot of my bed, waiting for Grady's call. She's always done that. If anything went amiss, she'd be dressed and ready to go and pick Grady up or maybe drive back all the way to where they had held the Crusade to get his things if he had to leave unexpectedly for another place. Why, I don't think Grady Wilson could make it at all—at least not with his luggage or at the right time and the right place—without Wilma, along with the help of his wonderful secretary, Aileen Shouse.

And let me tell you, Ethel Waters wouldn't want to try to make it without Grady and Wilma Wilson, either.

Another way my precious Lord takes care of me and is teaching me about love and has from the first time I was asked to sing "Sparrow" at the New York Crusade is where my music family is concerned . . . I really don't know one note from another. That's a fact. And I have a funny range as musicians understand that kind of thing. I can go low and I can go high—but I do both instinctively. Right now, although I can't go high like I once could, I can go down to what they tell me is F below Middle C. So, when Cliff Barrows asked me to sing "Sparrow" long ago, I had to explain to Tedd Smith, the Crusade pianist, that I sing in funny keys. I told Tedd that everybody can't play for me. You see, unless I hear particular chords I'm sunk. I said that it had to be just a certain way, so Tedd said he'd do all he could to help.

All of my long professional career as a singer, I've been thankful that musicians—the ones that played my accompaniment—seemed to like me. You know, many singers want to hog it and don't want the musician accompanying to do anything except back 'em up and let *them* make all the noise. They don't give the musician a chance to execute nothing. But with me, my accompanists inspire me, so my arrangements always had something that really *sell* the accompanist too. This inspires them. I tried to explain all this to Tedd, but in explaining it to him—to anybody—I have to tell more about one of the best musicians in the world, my darling Reggie Beane. On his own, Reginald Beane is a renowned composer, pianist, performer, and actor. He's really a classical musician. He's studied it. He knows it all. He was the arranger and accompanist for the Channing Choir and the Eva Jessye Chorus during the run of the Theater Guild's *Porgy and Bess*. Reggie was on radio with all kinds of variety shows, and he had a part in the Broadway play I starred in, *Mamba's Daughters*. He sings too. So he knows what I'm up against. He knows *me*. Nobody can top Reggie with me because he's just *it*. And I oughta know, since Reggie and I have been working together now for almost thirty-five years! He was just a child when we started out. But like my blessed old friend, Pearl Wright, now passed, Reggie *knew* what he was doing. It wasn't all instinct as with me. The same used to be true of Fletcher Henderson when he played for me. He had studied serious music too. And before any of these three fine musicians got with me, they looked down on what I did, the kind of music I sang. They all cultivated a liking for my music from working with me. I taught them to like the type of things I sang.

Reggie worked, oh, how he worked, with my half-brother, Johnny Waters. Now, Johnny Waters couldn't read music, just as I can't, but his improvisation was something! He could make his fingers talk. That boy could just play *everything*. So I'd get Johnny to come over in the early phases of my association with Reggie and Johnny would show him. Lots of the licks Reggie knows so well, he got from Johnny Waters. Today, of course, they're *writing* the same licks into music. But at that time, good licks weren't written down. They came from my people like Johnny Waters. You see, it was "by ear" music. The ear-music pianist *created* it. All those arrangements of my old stuff, now taken for granted among musicians in the secular world, were once ear-music from the neighborhoods like where I lived. Real lowdown. I transmitted it to these educated pianists for my own use.

I'd hum licks and things to Reggie and eventually, like a rabbit returning to its hole, it got so all I'd have to do was say, "Now, Reggie, I want you to z-z-z-z-z like that—" and he'd know exactly what I meant! He knew, because the music was in him and he knew and understood me musically and artistically. To this day, when I have anything coming up really difficult, I can still call on my baby, Reggie Beane.

Well, I told Tedd Smith about Reggie and that Reggie and I had *dum-de-dummed* it together for so long, that he knows what every little look means. So Tedd Smith was kind enough, bless his heart, to come to my suite back there in 1957 at the Empire Hotel, and over the phone, he got it straight from Reggie. He would play the chords Reggie told him right there on the piano I still have, then jot them down—the chords I would want to hear when I sang. The ones I was used to hearing and the key I sang it in whenever I'd sung "Sparrow" with Reggie, which I had so many times.

You see how my precious Saviour looked after that musical thing with me on the Crusades? Everyone on the Crusades knows and understands, not only how dependent I am physically, but also how completely I depend upon my musicians. And the Crusades all have top musicians. They're the real thing. They've all studied and they all know.

First and foremost, to me, my child, Cliff Barrows, is just a marvelous musical director. I don't see how he gets such good music out of so many people on such short notice. He's just wonderful. And has always been so very kind to me. Except—and he'll know I'm laughing when I say this—that blessed boy has a way of just sending me up the wall. He'll say, when I'm just about ready to begin to sing, "Take your time, Ethel, but keep it moving!" Now, how can I take my time and keep it moving all at once? But from the first, Cliff has been such a comfort and such a help to me.

I'm partial to the organ for the simple reason that I don't have much breath left. You only have to listen to me talk to know that.

I have to repeat words when I sing, to fill in, and the organ sustains and carries the melody for me. I'm Mom to all of the Crusade musicians—John Innis, Ted Cornell, Don Hustad, and Eddie Thomas. They tease me and kid me and I hand it right back. I couldn't do without them. I can get right off a plane and without any rehearsal, step onto the platform, lean up against the podium, and begin to croak. They're right under me, filling in, making it sound great. Without realizing it much of the time, they're all making me comfortable working among my new Christian family.

Jesus sends these musical ravens to feed me because He knows how much I need them. Nobody among these children gets paid any more for giving Mom Waters that little extra. More than they could ever guess, they're helping me learn to believe that people love me for *myself,* not because I have what the public calls a name. They are all His children, too, and He knows how helpless I am without someone "underneath" to "comfort" me when I sing. I don't consider that I *sing* a piece of music. I recite musically. I'm what I would call a *delineator of song.* What I think of as singing must have a tonal quality I feel I always lacked. If I'd known how to protect my voice, I might have been a singer. But when I first started out, I worked in spots where they had any kind of piano plunker and most likely he could only play in one or two keys—either too high or too low, so I strained my voice. But with my musician children now, I'm supported by the love of God along with the music and I'm grateful.

My wonderful Lord knew how alone I'd always been. He knew I needed the family kind of Christian love I experience wherever I travel. He knew all about Waters' rough edges and that nothing smooths out those rough edges like learning how to take down your guard and begin to *receive* love. God's love. Jesus knew, too, that even though I'd lived in Los Angeles a long time, I needed a family there for the time in between Crusades and other engage-

ments. Remember, He sent me Wils and Donna Wilson for when
I was so fat and so sick. I hope our sharing a home together was
a blessing to them, as it was to me. But now that I live alone, I'm
still not without a family here in Los Angeles. You see, the Lord
also knows how forgetful I can be, how I lose addresses and
telephone numbers and misspell checks. So, along with Bill Brown
and his wife, Joan, He has sent my precious child, Bill's secretary,
Twila Knaack, to help keep me out of trouble and at the right
airport when I'm supposed to be there. Twila goes shopping with
me, makes the cutest outfits for me now and then, sometimes even
helps me bathe when I'm not feeling too well. Bill Brown is important to me for more than sawing off the arm of that chair back
at the New York Crusade. Through him, Twila came into my life
and oh, we do have a ball together. Bill and Joan and Twila and
West Coast friends like Bootsie and Joe Howard, Cy and Vee
Jackson, and Hal Riddle help keep me on an even keel most of
the time. I think they dig me. Anyway, we laugh a lot and they
give me the kind of family love I always longed for. They let me
feel as independent as I want to feel (and I still am!), but they
also let me feel included in the circle of their loving care and devotion.

I don't think Cy Jackson knew it, but I was on the verge of
learning a big lesson through him the first time he called me right
after the New York Crusade when I came back to Christ. Cy was
then producing *Music for America* in Denver and he asked me
to sing for him. He wasn't a friend yet and I gave him a hard time,
just like I gave George Wilson the first time he called. I was so
new in the Christian life that I was really mixed up as to what to
say to Cy. He explained that *Music for America* wasn't like what
I would think of as secular. That lots of Christians sang on it.
He even gave me their names. But it wasn't Billy and I was scared
to say Yes.

Now, while I was living with my children, Donna and Wils
Wilson, soon after I began to take off weight, I did a run in *The*

*Member of the Wedding*—a very successful run at the Pasadena Playhouse. But I never have felt *Member* to be wrong for me because, you remember, I changed the interpretation of my role of Berenice Sadie Brown and certainly singing "Sparrow" glorifies God.

But there I was on long distance with Cy Jackson from Denver, all mixed up about what he was asking me to do and oh, he had a battle with me! I still sometimes have to ponder and wonder about taking this engagement or that—you see, if I say Yes, then I get scared for fear it isn't right. Back then, when poor Cy was trying to convince me, I was worse about it than now. I loved Jesus Christ so much and I was so happy that He took me back all the way, I would have *starved* before I'd knowingly done something that might in any way hurt Him. When Cy told me of other Christians singing on *Music for America,* that didn't impress me much either. You see, I didn't want to be one of God's children who used something decent like *Music for America* as a springboard! You can do that. You can accept work on something that's really all right, but still be doing it to spread yourself abroad in order to get more jobs. I've seen so many people use things like that as an angle, a pitch to get in—just because it wasn't dirty. So I told Cy that if I hadn't been on the level about rededicating my life to Christ, I could have gone back to my former work. I could still be singing "Stormy Weather" and "Dinah," but I meant business with Jesus. I told Cy I didn't have to compromise. I wasn't washed up in my old profession. Far from it. I didn't have to do halfway things.

Poor Cy talked and he talked and he talked. Said I would be the main attraction. That didn't move me. I'd been that too long. Said he was making the offer *because* a whole new audience of people, Christians, would want to hear me after I had sung "Sparrow" at the Crusade in New York. The Spirit witnessed in me that Cy Jackson was on the level. That he was a Christian, but I just couldn't be sure it was right for me to jump back into something

I had any doubts about. He'd told me the program. It was all right. It was nice. And while Cy kept talking, I said, "Oh, Lord, I don't know what to do! Help me." Finally, right then, I calmed down and I told Cy he'd just have to call me back.

I thought and thought. And what happened then, happens today if Ethel will just stop talking and get quiet before the Lord. That still small voice will come through to me and my Jesus knows that to the best of my ability, that's the one I listen to. In a minute, something said, "Why can't you go there and sing 'Sparrow'? That's all they're asking. After all, it's the same song you sang at the Crusade." I began to weigh things and I learned something. I could sing just as well for Jesus up in the Rocky Mountains as at a Crusade! I hadn't tried to convince Cy. He was the one trying to convince me. I wasn't out beatin' the bushes trying to find a big spot for Ethel Waters to sing "in His name" just for Ethel Waters. I wasn't. God knew I wasn't. But it took me a long time to get all this straight. I don't question it anymore even when I *know* other people are doing it. He sees it too. I just worry about Waters. But it can turn you off, if you're a beginner, to see God's work used for a commercial angle. It hasn't been easy for me to get to this place, and I wasn't there when I told my darling Cy Jackson that I'd reconsidered and would come to Denver to sing "Sparrow." I was still crawling then. Through the years, I've seen a lot of things, but I just keep my eyes on Jesus. Even when they begin tempting me with "no harm to sing this, no harm to sing that." I tell you, Hell's going to be full of "no harm" Christians. Oh, boy, they're going to have to build an annex. There'll be standing room only!

Cy knows all about that call now, bless his heart, and he understands. He and Vera have become my dear friends. They know that down through the years when people *have* tried to tempt me into singing a song I shouldn't, I just shake my head and say, Nope. When they say, "But it would be so nice if you sang so and so." Nope. Just "Sparrow." Oh, I'll sing "Cabin in the Sky," too, like when I sang "Sparrow" and "Cabin" on Pearl Bailey's TV show in 1971.

Now don't get me wrong. There's no harm in Christians *asking* me to sing something else besides hymns or songs about Jesus and heaven. But Waters is trying to keep everything clear with God in her own heart, so why should she sing something she don't feel right about?

Jesus said you can't follow God and mammon. And singing songs like "St. Louis Blues" and "Heat Wave" and shaking my hips and making a whole lot of money *is* mammon to me. That's what all that means to Ethel Waters. I'm not saying it can't be done by somebody else, but not by Waters. *I have relinquished all that.*

Do you remember what Jesus said to the rich young ruler? He didn't say the boy was necessarily sinning by being rich. But the boy had told Jesus that he wanted to follow *Him*! The Lord knew what all that money meant to the young ruler, so He told him what he'd have to give up. Ethel Waters wanted to follow Jesus. She *wanted* to follow Jesus so therefore He told her what she'd have to give up in order to do that. Singing secular songs was not only my livelihood, it was all I had. I gave it up and I was sincere. So, I still thank my precious Lord for friends who understand and who know what the central issue is with me.

A very important member of my West Coast family is my wonderful Dr. Jack Scheinkopf, whom I trust. This means a lot when you're not well and getting along in years as I am. Dr. Scheinkopf is my friend. He's proven that. Ever since he first saw me stacked up in that hospital bed—all 380 pounds of me—hardly able to get my breath. He didn't have to go out of his way, but I know he did many times. He'd come back at night and just sit and talk to me and comfort me. Not like a professional call, more that he wanted to make sure I was all right for that night. Although the Saviour is the head physician, He also provides earthly people to see to your physical and material needs and your comfort. All of these loving people are under His direction. My part of it is to give out love to them as best I can, because I've learned that if you give out love, you get back love. Jesus bands people together in a Christian bond. I'm in His union now and you don't pay no dues in His union. It's the heart that's the fee. Love belongs to Him and He spreads it all out so there's more than we all need.

# Part Four

I was bitter as well as lonesome for Jesus when I rededicated my life to Him back at the 1957 New York Crusade. And the big reason *then* for my painful bitterness was that I was so *fat*.

I hated my size and I had grown bitter about it. Not so much because I knew I didn't look good anymore—I wasn't bitter because I'd lost my good figure—but because all my life I had been an *active* person with no need to be size conscious. I was always fairly immune to flattery. A handshake if it was sincere meant more than a eulogy.

Of course, seeing that weight begin to pile on, I adored the sweat baths and massages I began to take, but it was then I found out to my horror that I had built up a solid *fat foundation*. I also discovered that fat is like a fungus, you can remove the top layer, but the bottom remains dormant, and is the hardest and last to go.

As the pounds piled on, I found I was having terrible difficulty doing just the ordinary things, and my bitterness grew faster than the fat. I'd try to diet and I'd take those steam baths and massages, but by the time I was in my late fifties, I believed I would just have to endure and learn to adjust to this terrible affliction. Never having had to give a thought to my weight, it sneaked up on me. My bitterness became almost a second handicap. It turned to out-and-out *hatred* when it seemed everybody went out of their way to tell me how fat I was.

I hated and I was bitter. Part of what bugged me was having

*closets* (plural) *full of expensive complete outfits* and then ending up at Lane Bryant's to hunt something I could get into. And sometimes even they didn't have my size! The woes of becoming a fat, middle-aged woman with no previous experience at coping with the menace of an unwieldy body are horrible. It seemed to me it had all happened overnight. Of course, it didn't, but learning to live with it was a brand new experience when I reached the place where I was getting in my own way.

Now, I had always been the type of person to face facts, and one day I decided to *force* myself to open one of those well-filled closets, select a dress and try it on. I should have said *try* to try it on, because there I stood in front of a full-length mirror stuck part way into that small-sized dress and what I saw was so *grotesque,* I got to laughing and couldn't stop. That was *before* Billy's Crusade in 1957, but I know the moment of laughter was my heavenly Father's way—with one stroke—of winning that battle. As I stood there laughing, I faced the truth about what had really happened to me and instantly the hatred and bitterness began to drain away. The fat didn't drain away in an instant, let me tell you, but I had my rose-tinted glasses *off* and was seeing myself as I really was: a big fat, middle-aged, gray-haired woman. *Overstuffed*. I also faced what I had been told, that fat doesn't stand still. It is constantly multiplying and this is the Voice of Experience speaking!

I was not a professing Christian then, although I had always talked to God when I was alone, but as I stood there looking so grotesque and laughing so hard at myself, I could feel the warmth of His smile.

Looking at fat, aging Ethel Waters in that full-length mirror, and laughing, my mind went back to when I was a child and laughed and thought certain old folks were funny—what they did, what they wore—especially if they were fat! Back in those days people were themselves and didn't put on so many airs. The children laughed at the old folks' get-ups and certain funny things they did. Still you had to mind and obey them because they were grown-ups. At least you did to their faces, but that didn't stop you from having some pretty ornery thoughts even though you really loved them.

I thought first of old Aunt Betsy, whom I dearly loved, but who was no relation. She lived in a one-room rear house and oh, she was *fat* and she dipped snuff, so she was always drooling. Aunt Betsy wore about four petticoats, a thick skirt, a blouse, a man's sweater and a starched apron. I loved to be around her when I was seven or eight just to watch the expert way she could aim and never miss when she would *skeet* that snuff. (Meaning to a younger generation that she could spit a great distance and never miss.) Aside from her expert *skeeting,* Aunt Betsy was also a midwife, so one day when she was out delivering a baby, I decided to try to skeet the way she did. I opened her snuffbox and poured some in the lid the way I'd seen her do it, then I pulled down my bottom lip and began to pour it in. I must have had too much in the lid or was shaking too hard, because I ended up with snuff in my mouth, up my nose, my eyes burning, and instead of *skeeting* I was swallowing! I made a B-line for the outhouse and sick as a yellow dog, I begged the Lord to please forgive me and also not to let Aunt Betsy or my own Aunt Vi find out what I'd done!

Still standing in front of that mirror with that small-sized dress on as far as it would go, I thought, "You're a lot like Aunt Betsy! You can skeet (water) through your teeth and you're getting old and your hair is gray—and you're *fat.*"

I wiggled out of that skimpy dress, but my memory didn't get free. I thought next of Aunt Kate, another old lady I knew and loved when I was a child and Aunt Kate ate starch! And *she* was fat. Always all her pockets were full of starch and she chewed it with such relish, I decided I'd have to give that a try too. Well, it tasted blah! That didn't stop me. I would cultivate a taste for it if it killed me. And it nearly did, because after three days I was so constipated, my Aunt Vi and Aunt Ching thought I had locked bowels, not knowing what I'd been eating. My aunts were scared half to death. So once more I beseeched the Lord to help me and give me some relief. With the aid of Epsom Salts, Castor Oil, and a soap enema—all of which gave immediate action—I felt the Lord had answered my prayers all right. He'd overdone it!

I walked away from that full-length mirror, wrapped in something loose, and sat thinking about those old people I used to laugh at. We didn't mean them no harm when we laughed at them because they dressed funny and were *fat*. I guess we thought we'd earned the right to a private laugh or two, since in those days youngsters were expected to help elderly people, especially if they were sick or very old and unable to do for themselves.

Today, in telling this, I'm realizing all over again that the same thing has, in a way, happened to me. Didn't I tell you Twila has to help me take my bath sometimes? And can I even walk across a platform without someone's arm to support and steady me? There's a saying: The same dog that bit you, snapped at me. Oh, boy, lots of times I had to rub Aunt Betsy's swollen old feet. Well, *my* feet swell sometimes. Another reason we had to help Aunt Betsy and Aunt Kate when we were children was because they were too fat to help themselves! We'd have to help them bathe and there weren't any tubs either. When they'd ask us to help them wash themselves, we'd have to use a big pail to sponge their big old fat arms and the rolls of fat at the back of their necks. As children, we thought their fat was funny!

I wasn't standing by that mirror anymore. I'd had enough. But I could still see myself and I said, "Lord, Lord, I look just like fat old Aunt Betsy! Aunt Ethel Waters is a mess! She *tops* Aunt Betsy."

Still chuckling at myself, I was sure then that the tension and the bitterness had been broken in me, but I remembered another saying that "whatever goes over the Devil's back has got to come under his belly." Nobody should laugh at anybody because it can come back on you—like chickens comin' home to roost.

You see, when I was a child, I had no weight problem. Sometimes I didn't have enough to eat, but if we had food, I could eat a ton without giving it a thought. That was true until my late fifties, when I began to inflate like a big old balloon. Even though it didn't all come on as fast as it seemed to me, I was just not in any way accustomed to fat, to the handicap of a cumbersome body. Don't laugh at a fatty. They're *handicapped*. But if they've grown up with fat, at least they know something about how to handle themselves. What to expect. What not to try to do! I didn't. It frightened me. I felt so helpless so much of the time before and for the months after my rededication to Christ, I would cry out to Him, pleading for Him to help me learn to adjust, just to handle myself in everyday things. It's a miserable feeling to go to somebody's house, sit down in a chair, and the chair breaks! It isn't funny. It's tragic.

I got to the place where I was afraid to sit down, and I was too tired and too big to stand up. I would get on a plane, and the first time that happened, I remember, I didn't know to ask for an extension belt and the seat belt wouldn't go around me and I was panic-stricken! I finally learned from a nice little stewardess that they had extension belts for corpulent people, but once I remember they didn't have one and had to hold the plane while they sent somebody to get one that would go across my fat stomach. Another time, there wasn't an extension belt to be found, so the pilot had to make an easy landing because there I sat without a belt!

I've told you about those early days when my children at the Crusades would so kindly let me come just to be with them and to hear Billy preach. Of course, I was still so terribly big and would be so miserable they would have a doctor available at whatever city I joined them and he would give me medication. Different women members of the Crusades and the wives of the Team boys helped me rest enough so I could sing, or at least sit up long enough to hear my child, Billy, preach. You know I *longed* to be fed spiritually, or in my miserable condition both during the

Crusade in New York and in those first months afterward, I would never have made the effort to get there.

I've always been conscious of what I wear, too. I don't think I was a clothes horse, but I didn't like to wear anything that wasn't right and I was then just big all over—but bigger in the stomach! Buying anything to wear was like a bad dream I had to live through. One day I got a bright idea. I'd looked at some pictures of what I thought were very smart outfits for large women. Then I realized they were maternity dresses! But they were sharp. So one day I was standing in front of the window of a beautiful shop where they had on display all these dresses for pregnant women. I hadn't gone in yet. I was just standing near the door still looking in the window. I said, "Lord, they sure look good, don't they?" And about that time a saleslady noticed me with my huge stomach and she came to the open door of the shop and said, "If we don't have your size, madame, we can order it."

I looked at her, then I thought to myself, "Nothing but a try beats a failure. I might as well go in there and try!" After all, I knew *mine* was permanent.

And do you know, I got the cutest dress that covered how big my stomach was? I did, and it looked so good, I could wear it to a Crusade and I did! There I was, sashayin' around all dressed up. I've never told this story on myself before, but it's true.

It's true and it's funny.

When I was touring with Cy Jackson and *Music for America* during that same big fat period, they had to work around and find a mike I could hang around my neck because my big stomach kept me too far away from the floor mike. There was *no way* to get the mike close enough to me as it would pick up my voice right. That big stomach took up just too much room for sound transmission. I had decided I'd do fine though if I could just lean into the curve of the piano to sing. I *had* to touch something because I was so ill from that fat around my heart, I never knew when I was going to fall. And if I fell, who could get me up? I stood in the

wings too, until it was my time to come on, because I was afraid
to sit down. I refused, even when they worried about my getting
too tired and running short of breath. I refused. I just said, "Cy,
I can't do it!" I'd have been too emotionally upset to sing, so I'd
breathe, "Lord, please don't make me have to sit down! Please!"

I did all right singing, leaning there in the curve of the piano,
touching it with my hand to steady myself, until at one curtain
call, something happened in the line-up of the cast and somebody
else got into my curve in that piano for the finale. Bless the Lord,
I had to stand out in front! I stood there because there wasn't any-
place else to stand. I couldn't suddenly shift the whole cast around
in front of all those people. But when the curtain started down, and
they saw it coming and me standing out there in front, they
shifted all right! Oh, they started moving fast, because there was
just no way—they knew it and I knew it—for that heavy curtain
to get past my stomach!

The audience got the message, and to coin a phrase, "It was
fantastic!"

Now, I've told some of these funny things about my own fat—
for whom it may concern. If you're not fat yet—don't. If you're fat,
get it off, or it can kill you. I know.

How did I get it off? Almost 200 pounds? I stayed under my
doctor's care and prayed to my heavenly Father to help me. He did.

I'm still paying the price of that fat, even though a lot of it's
gone. But my heart is bad, I have diabetes, and have to watch my
blood pressure which got up to 260 over 180 when I weighed so
much. I lived. I'm still pitchin', but I'm damaged goods, in spite of
the fact that I *never* smoked or drank. Not even in my old life.
Since some members of my family liked it (not my mother, rest
her soul), I just wasn't going to drink. I was going to prove that
what your family does, you don't have to do. You know how people
say, "Well, she's from *that* family . . ." and they say it sort of
behind their hand. I showed them. I just didn't drink at all. I'd

work in clubs and sit with guests or with friends and drink milk. Wine and champagne taste like the vinegar and water I used to take for an upset stomach. I never had wine and I don't have it now. It's hard to make the people on a plane believe you don't want their champagne-dinner, that you just want some of the dinner. But I surely wouldn't drink it under the table if I wanted some. The Lord would see if I swallowed it. Anyway, why swallow something you don't like when you don't have to? I don't tell anybody else not to drink. I just have to account for Waters. And I try to take care of myself now—what's left of me.

You see, even without that 200 pounds, traveling is still hard. Not frightening the way it was when I was so terribly big, because then I'd nearly collapse trying to walk through a city airport. I can't take those long walks now. I have to be pushed in a wheel chair, because my legs become like lead and I get very close to fainting. When I've tried it, I've just sunk to the floor. But I don't say much about any of this. Everything gets distorted when it's told by word of mouth. People exaggerate and make my condition sound so sensational. Instead, when I'm behind closed doors alone, I talk to Jesus about it. I tell Him my needs. I ask Him to support me and have someone there to push my chair and help me with my luggage.

I *know* He's going to give me strength to make a joyful noise, so I thank Him in advance. But this is the straight of it: Sometimes when I'm sitting there on a Crusade platform, my heart is pounding and thumping so loud, I can almost hear it! I tremble something terrible and it's not stage fright. It's my condition. I'm nervous. Then after I've sung, when I'm sitting there with my children, they can see me shaking. But never, never when I'm up singing! Then you don't detect anything wrong. Not *anything*. I'm just as still as a calm breeze all through my number. And I'm grateful for that. People don't come to sympathize or hear your complaints, they come to hear you deliver, and the way I can be in control while I'm singing is the reason many take my physical condition so lightly.

But when people are traveling on the same plane with me, they know. Travel is fast, but it's hard, partly because it does all go so fast. But I receive love and courtesy most of the time and I try to keep love in my heart. Jesus is there and He's love, so all I have to do when I'm tired or not feeling well is just keep myself reminded that He's there and I have all the love I need for those around me on planes or in cars or airports.

I was on a big plane once when a man got on who was pretty far gone from drinking. The stewardess hesitated to let him sit beside me, but I didn't. I said to let the poor fellow sit right down. Finally, when he got around to talking to me, I could see he was just all to pieces. Of course, they wouldn't give him another drink even though he wanted one, but he was in bad shape. I could tell he had a terrible problem of some kind. He looked so miserable.

"Why don't you eat something, child?" I asked him.

"I don't wanna eat. I wan' another drink."

I said, "But drinking hasn't solved your problem, why not try some food instead?"

He just looked at me.

"You've been smoking one cigarette after another ever since the plane got off the ground. Soon as one goes out, you light another and that hasn't helped either."

He looked so unhappy, so distressed, but he didn't answer. He just looked at me. I went on, "I don't know what your problem is, but I know you can be helped. I *know* it."

He turned in his seat and asked, "What's your name?"

"My name's Ethel Waters."

"*You*—Ethel Waters?"

"Yes."

"*The* Ethel Waters?"

"*Just* Ethel Waters."

After a few seconds he asked me where I was going, and I told him I was going to a Crusade. Then he told me his name and began to get very serious, like a troubled little boy.

Finally, he said, "There's something about you reminds me of someone very close—a woman who helped raise me. You're just like her."

The poor fellow, whose name I forget, except that his nickname was Red, told me the name of the woman who'd raised him was Tempy. She'd looked after him from the time he was a baby and I reminded him of her, so he began then to tell me about his horrible burden. He was going to bury his daughter, who had been a beautiful musician. She had called him to come to a certain concert she was giving and he didn't go. Now he was heartsick. His lovely daughter had been killed in an automobile accident.

I tried to let him know that I understood and that I cared about him, but he was in no condition for a lot of talk. I then told him I wanted him to eat something and not take one more drink. "After you've had some food to soak up that liquor, I want you to put your head on my shoulder and take a nap. That way you'll be able to face what's up ahead. When you get off this plane, whoever meets you will know you're—a *man.*"

He looked at me again and said, "Lord, that's just the way Tempy would have said it!"

When he had sat down, he was loud and boisterous. I understood why he was. He was striking out at life because of his hurt, his hideous pain. That was natural. He had the crew and the other passengers all concerned that he was going to annoy everybody for the whole trip. I sensed that what he needed was comfort. I'd needed comfort myself for so long and never found it until I found Jesus. They brought the food, he ate, and in no time he had dropped his head on my shoulder and he slept like a baby for at least an hour and a half.

My shoulder got a little kinked sitting in one position, but I wouldn't have shifted around for anything. I just sat there and said, "Lord, let this child sleep—let him sleep."

As I recall, we were changing planes in Atlanta. I asked the stewardess for a cold, wet towel and then I woke him up when I saw we were almost there. He wiped his face off good, combed his hair, looked me straight in the eye and said, soberly now, "I *do* want to thank you."

I patted his hand. "Honey, thank the Lord. He knew what you needed right then. Now you go on and get off this plane and meet your aunt or your sister, or whoever, and don't you take another drink. Don't waste your strength trying to thank me. You'll need it all. The Lord knew you needed some rest and He found this shoulder. You just needed a shoulder when you got on this plane. And whenever you look to Him, He's always going to let you find a shoulder when you need it. You see, son, there are more Tempys around."

I was glad I hadn't lost too much weight. That boy needed a good shoulder. But daily, I'm grateful to be rid of both the weight and my bitterness. Bitter people have trouble seeing beauty. I'm glad I have room and space inside me now to see and enjoy all the natural beauty I get to see traveling around with the Crusades. Especially when I'm with Grady, we just live it up looking at trees! I appreciate trees. Why, they almost talk to you. I can feel their gigantic strength and I love to look up at them towering there against the sky. Don't forget I grew up in a dirty, smelly alley and I just can't seem to get enough of God's beauty. Those trees and mountains and rivers make me so thankful for my eyesight. Oh, boy, I don't want no blinds and curtains to cover up what I can still see. There might be a time comin' when I can't see, so I want to look now.

If I don't look too long, it's not so bad to catch a glimpse of Waters these days. At least she doesn't resemble Aunt Kate anymore.

# Part Five

When I have a long wait between planes, sometimes it gets rough. The sky cap pushes my wheel chair to the gate where the next plane leaves, and there's nothing to do but sit and remain in that chair. Especially if it's the kind of chair you can't operate yourself! It gets really rough when the next plane is two or three hours late and you're by yourself. The sky cap's got other tips to make until it's time to come back to push you to where you're finally going.

Now, I always try to go prepared, if you get my point, but even though all modern airports *claim* they have centrally located rest rooms, don't let them kid you! If you're sitting in a wheel chair at Gate 61, that "conveniently located" rest room is going to be at Gate 37, which is several miles *back!* I try to anticipate this, but how can anybody anticipate when a plane's going to be three hours late? There come times when you desperately want a drink of water. The drinking fountain, the nearest one, that is, is several miles *back* too. After awhile, you want to wash your hands and so on And there you sit, stranded. You wait and you sit and you hope and then you pray. The Devil is there with you and he makes you want that drink of water and so on—I mean *desperately.*

I'm laughing now, but it's no laughing matter at the time. This once, in particular, there I sat in my wheel chair and after a few minutes, I called to a man who was sweeping up. I said, "*Sir,* where is the ladies lounge?" (I addressed him as Sir. My second childhood has made me polite!) He answered, "Oh, it's way down —way down that way." He spoke so funny, I didn't believe him. Even for an airport, that seemed too far away. I said, "You mean *way* down there?" And he said, "Yeah, *way* down there." Then he went back to sweeping without coming a step closer. (Pushing me for money would undoubtedly have been wrong—the wrong union!) I don't think he heard me, but I said, "Thank you."

After awhile another maintenance man came by and once more I said pleadingly, "Sir? Could you *please* tell me approximately how far it would be to the nearest ladies lounge?" He went on sweeping, but I could understand him better, the way he talked, and he assured me he didn't know what they were thinking about when they built the place, but that the *nearest* ladies lounge was halfway back to the terminal!

All I said to him was "Oh!" and he went on with his work. Finally, because I talk to the Lord about everything, I said, "What am I going to do, Lord? I've still got almost two hours to wait for that plane!" I began to wonder if I could possibly make it there and back by easing myself along near enough to the wall so I could touch it and steady myself while I walked. "Do you think, Lord Jesus, that I can get there and back and not miss that plane? I know I can't wait for no two hours!"

I sat there for another minute or so and I had my answer. I *had* to try!

I pulled myself up out of that chair, left my tote bag on the seat, and began slowly, *slowly* walking along the side where I could keep touching the wall with one hand. Praying, "Lord, give me the strength and don't let me buckle! I've just got to try and make it!"

As anyone such as my darling Twila Knaack knows, because she helps me so much and goes so many places with me, I not only have to touch something, but also I have to sort of tighten myself up when I have to walk any distance. I get out of breath so fast if I don't, I'm panting before I know it. So I'd walk a ways, then I'd try to look casual as I stopped at one little cubby hole or another along the corridor to rest. Well, that man with the broom was right! It was *way* down. It looked like the farther I walked, the farther away that sign moved. But I kept at it, praying to the Lord with every step and stopping often to catch my breath and rest my legs. And you don't have to believe this, but seven, *seven* times, while I was stopped or about to stop again for a breather, people came running up to me to ask if I was Ethel Waters! Some of them practically punched me when they'd say, "Could *you* be Ethel Waters? Oh, I wish I weren't in such a hurry" or "I wish I had a piece of paper so I could get your autograph!" I'm glad if they like me, but Twila or anybody who has ever seen me struggle to walk any distance by myself can tell you, I don't look like I'm in any condition to sign autographs! Anybody, *anybody* could see I wasn't up to par, that I was having a hard time. But do you think any of those "fans" who ran up offered to help me?

When I was about, oh, fifty or sixty feet from that sign I'd been heading for, a nice-looking businessman stopped and said, "I'd be glad to get a wheel chair and push you wherever you're going, lady." I tried to smile and I thanked him, but said I was almost there and pointed at the sign. He tipped his hat and walked away.

I made it. And just as I was coming back out the door of the ladies lounge, here came that same lovely businessman with one of the airline clerks in tow who had pointed out my chair and bag. They were hurrying toward me, pushing my wheel chair! The man wasn't allowed, I learned later, to up and push one without an employee with him, and while I was in the lounge, he had talked the clerk into accompanying him so I wouldn't have to fight my way back to the gate again. To this day, with my memory, I'd probably pass that wonderful man and not know him and I never did get his name, but the part that made me so happy was that he did *not* know my name, either! He had gone to the bother of finding out the regulations on wheel chairs and had come all that way back to help me. That's how close he was observing my condition and my struggle. Not the autograph seekers, though. All they thought was they wished they'd had the time or a piece of paper. You see, I won't ask for help unless it seems right to me, and it didn't seem right with either one of those maintenance men or the seven people who wanted Ethel Waters' autograph! I thanked that dear man profusely and blessed him. I might not have made it all the way back without him. I could have scrubbed that man's floors.

Another time I had been with my child, Leighton Ford, on a Crusade in Canada. I was to leave on a certain night to be with Billy at another Crusade in North Carolina, and when I left Leighton in Canada, it was a beautiful night. Clear and starry. But when the plane landed wherever it was we had to change, bless the Lord, it was cold and storming so hard it was nearly blowing the housetops away. It was terrible!

Of course, I expected someone to meet me with a wheel chair (I've logged a lot of miles in those things!) but the poor girl who was to meet me couldn't get from the terminal to where the plane was parked in that storm. I'm tellin' you, that wind was howlin' and things were blowin' around the field and the rain was comin' down in buckets. I just sat there on the plane in my seat and waited. I knew I had to make my connection to get to North Carolina, but the girl knew she could never hold an umbrella and that the wind could just plain knock her over too. She managed to get word to me on the plane through the crew, and then everybody began to wonder how in the world they were going to get me off and into that terminal.

While all this wondering was going on, the fellow drove up with his truck that delivered coffee and food and so forth. He got into the conversation aboard the plane about me and my predicament. As he talked with the stewardesses, I learned that this particular man wasn't even supposed to be working that shift that night. He was taking another fellow's turn. I didn't pay much attention to that, though. All I was thinking was, "Lord, how are they going to get me all that long distance in this storm!"

Suddenly, I heard this food and coffee fellow say, "I'll take her straight over to her connecting flight on my truck!"

I still laugh so hard I almost cry when I tell this story, because on the other plane were the crew and the rest of them waiting eagerly in that cold and wet for their coffee and doughnuts—and when the door opened through which they were anticipating their refreshments—out I came! Those people on my connecting flight sure had startled looks on their faces when they saw me instead of the coffee and doughnuts.

Now, here's the payoff. The kind young man who delivered me instead of the coffee and doughnuts to my other plane broke a rule to do it. The whole crew told me that if the regular man had been on duty, he would never, never have broken the rule to help an old lady onto a plane!

You know Who worked this all out, don't you? To me, *He's wonderful*!

Sometimes when you travel you find sad things happening to you. Other times, touching, tender little incidents. But I just couldn't live if I didn't laugh and so maybe I go around looking for more than my share of funny happenings. I don't miss much. I never have. I might seem not to be looking or listening or paying any mind, but later, more than likely you'll find out I was digging it all the time!

Before I relate this little incident (which I decided to consider humorous), I'd better tell you that I've done everything in show business from carnivals to speakeasies to Hollywood to Broadway. Being an actor or an actress now is stylish. Society people are taking up acting (or what I'd call society people) and they're taking on roles to play which they couldn't possibly understand. I could never see how anyone could play a role which he or she didn't understand. But back in the old days when I was young, real theater performers were treated like slaves. Color had nothing to do with it. Acting was simply the lowest profession. If you were white or colored, you had to stay in the town's whorehouse or some similar environment, simply because you were an actor. There was just nothing lower. To church people, an actress was automatically a scarlet woman! But the rest of society excluded you as well. Yet, you were a performer, so you learned how to live with it.

Well, this funny incident I'm speaking of happened when I was in Lexington, Kentucky, with Billy in May of 1971. I'm telling you for a laugh and also to show you how people in a "sweet" way like to bring you down. Or show you they remember you "when."

I was invited with the rest of the Crusade Team by a lovely Christian couple to an affair at their gorgeous home. I mean, it is an estate. They have stables and everything. They're beautiful people *and* they're Southern. I've met a lot of loving, kind white Southerners and I like them, and if I like a white Southerner nobody's gonna button my lip! They can call me Aunt Tomasina or whatever, but there are some fine people in the South. Just like there are skunks in the North.

Well, these people brought me to their country place in their limousine and the place was truly beautiful, with lots of green grass and trees—*and* standing on the steps was one of my people in his white coat. He and I exchanged glances, but instead of giving me a hand up those steps, the white-coated "gentleman" reminded me that the first time he met me was forty years ago when I came to Lexington with a carnival!

I turned slightly toward him and said, "I certainly do remember. I came here with Rutherford's Greater Shows and we ballyhooed and we also slept in the stables!" Then I gave him a smile. "It was *nice,* sleeping in the hay."

Oh, we ain't ready yet. Plenty of us ain't ready.

It seems as though when Twila Knaack and I go shopping, something funny's just bound to happen. Whenever we go into a store, though, we're both primed to ignore. Sometimes we're laughing when we walk in, sometimes not. But we're set to ignore and to be polite. We walk up to a certain counter and there's a clerk—a white clerk, who hasn't recognized me as Ethel Waters. I don't go in as Ethel Waters. I just go in to get what I want. So this white clerk looks up and sees me, an elderly colored woman with a smartly dressed, attractive young white girl and Twila is being very attentive to me. Of course, the white clerk is puzzled, and the first thing she'll say to this colored woman whom she doesn't know—all the while looking *between* Twila and me—is "Yes? So and so and so and so." Just giving her usual spiel to a faceless stranger. Two faceless strangers. Remember now, I haven't gone into this store with a sign around my neck or a ring in my nose or a fancy fur coat or anything like that. I'll just have on a shawl or whatever's comfortable. The clerk will tell us that she doesn't have so and so and so and so, then I'll ask her about something else. "Well," she'll say, still not looking at me or Twila, "I'll see if we have that item in stock."

I say, "Twila, run around to that side of the counter and look."

The clerk says, "Oh, you won't find it over there, miss."

Her nose is still about halfway up in the air, you know. And after awhile, with Twila's help, I settle on something, ask the price, Twila writes out my check to keep me from spoiling it, I sign it, the clerk takes it, reads the signature, her eyebrows fly up and she exclaims, "*Ethel Waters!* Oh-h!"

And there I stand, the same elderly colored woman in her shawl.

Now, that's the *white* clerk. Next we go into another store and behind the counter stands a *colored* salesgirl. She'd call herself "black" I'm sure, but to me she's colored. Just like we all are. I'm standing same as before, with an attractive young white girl. The chances are that unlike the white clerk, this colored salesgirl wouldn't recognize my name. Some young ones don't. So, in a high, hopefully cultivated voice, she asks, "May I help you?"

Or she just might rephrase it a little and say, "What would you like, madame?"

Either way, it's in that "impressive" voice.

I tell her I'm just looking around to see if I can find what I want. I say this in a very quiet, subdued voice. Twila is trying to keep her face straight. The colored girl starts to walk away, then tosses back at me over her shoulder, "When you make up your mind, let me know." Or words to that effect.

Do you get the message?

What Twila and I "get" is that it's six of one and half a dozen of the other. Of course, there is another kind of clerk who treats you human. Color or fame make no difference—you're a person—a member of the *human* race.

Most people have *images* in their minds of what this one and that one will be like. They have an image of Billy Graham. *Their* image. And that image is shaped by the little *they* know about the person, seldom what the person is in real life. This is especially true of people in the public eye.

Years ago, my colored people evidently went to the movies I had made and it just so happened that in so many of those movies, I played aging, ill, or old people. A lot of the young colored, because they've seen those old movies of mine on TV in reruns, have an image of Ethel Waters as being even older than she is and more feeble! Twila and I got a big dose of that peculiar image they have of me one night.

You see, my people have a gimmick they use now of giving things *in your honor,* which is simply a way of getting you there so they can use your name to draw a crowd to make money at their affairs. Oh, they bear down on you! Anyway, I got an invitation to one of those big affairs where I was to be the *honored* guest. Most of the time now I say No, but they made it sound almost like a command performance, so I asked Twila to write and say I'd be there. I didn't want to go, Lord knows. But their invitation was worded in such a way that I couldn't figure an excuse to get out of it.

Well, Twila and I got ready to go on this certain Saturday night to a Hilton Hotel, where the big affair was to be. I was very tired and kept saying, "Oh, dear Lord, I don't want to go to this thing. Lord, how did I ever happen to say I'd go?"

Twila looked very sweet and I had on a nice dress and we got to the Hilton and went inside, both of us knowing what a hard time I'd have making my way from one end of a long hotel like the Hilton to another. But we started our walk and, as usual, I moseyed along, pretending I was looking at this or that, so that it wouldn't show so much what a hard time I have walking. Those dressed-up colored folk passed me like freight trains passing a tramp.

Finally, we got outside the room where I thought we were supposed to be and stood there, but nobody paid us any mind. "Twila," I whispered, "what do we do next?" Then I saw somebody with one of those little tags on her dress, so I asked her about the proper entrance to the function. She glanced at me and said, "Oh, up there," and dashed off. After she was long gone, I mumbled, "Well, okay. Okay."

Inside the door of the dining room, they were frisking everybody, but the man looked at me and at least *honored* me by not bothering. Twila and I went in and in a minute or so, two beautifully groomed young ladies came up and looked me over. I was so tired by then, I was leaning hard on Twila. In a very soft, weary voice, I said, "I'm Ethel Waters. Who do I see?"

Still looking us over, one of them asked, "Who did you say you are?"

"Miss Waters."

"Well, just a moment."

Off they went and stayed, Twila and I still standing there, waiting. After awhile, four more came back, looked me over, and asked, "Who did you say you are?"

There I was, swaying on my feet from exhaustion—the "guest of honor" at their function to kick off whatever it was they were planning to kick off—and she repeated her question: "Who did you say you are?" Now, these were smart young ladies, intelligent, educated. They weren't handkerchief heads. So I repeated as patiently and in as ladylike a voice as I could manage at that point, "I—am—Miss Ethel Waters."

One of them cocked her head in a puzzled fashion and said, "Well, could you just wait here a few minutes?"

I waited, but only long enough to look straight back at her and then I said, "Look, baby, you just tell whoever it is you're supposed to tell that—Ethel Waters has been here—but now she's gone!"

It could be that those folks meant to honor me, they meant well, but they'd seen me dead or *half-dead* so often on the screen, they couldn't get it straight that I was still breathin'!

Along with the knocks and heartaches I've known in my seventy-six years, real honors have come to me too, and while there are some which had deep meaning for me, such as nominations for an Academy Award when I played Aunt Dicey in *Pinky* and the Emmy Award for a TV part, I've caught on long ago when a so-called "honor" means something. I don't know who they ended up praising that night at the Hilton, but it was a genuine honor to me when I was asked to go to Cleveland in March of 1971 when Billy Graham received the award from the National Conference of Christians and Jews. I felt honored and privileged and just plain happy being there with him that night. I remember I felt honored, too, that the distinguished critic Brooks Atkinson of *The New York Times* once wrote that in his opinion I should have received a Congressional Medal for my performance of Berenice Sadie Brown in *The Member of the Wedding* on Broadway. Well, I didn't, but twenty years later, I came by another Washington-type honor I'll never forget. In January of 1971 I was invited to sing at the Sunday Worship Service at the White House.

When I got to my hotel in the nation's capital, there was this nice note waiting from Deborah Murray, one of the President's staff, welcoming me to Washington and telling me that President and Mrs. Nixon would like me to join them for coffee before the service. I'd known the Nixons before, way back in the earlier part of Richard Nixon's career, right after my rededication to Christ when I sang in a lot of churches in California. I sang often at the Quaker church where his mother worshiped. I knew her and loved her and also her sister. This is no political plug, it is just fact that to me the Nixons are real people. I've liked him and his wife (I call her Patty Girl) since he was a congressman; during the time they were fighting him for assailing communism. That's when I got to like that man. They were accusing him of everything under the sun because he was beginning to hit where it hurt. I hate communism. I'd seen some of its evil effects during the years when the Communists were infiltrating show business in this country. I'm no witch hunter and I don't hate Communists, because they can change, but I hate communism. Richard Nixon has been fighting it a long time and I like him and believe in him. I knew Tricia and Julie when they were just little tykes, long before their daddy was famous. I had been in their home in California years ago.

I remember so well when Richard Nixon was running for governor in California after he lost his first presidential race. They were giving him a pretty hard time and he was awfully hurt. There are people in California who are good at crucifying a man and the time I'm speaking about now is when they were accusing Mr. Nixon of getting the Christian people to back him with a false statement or some such—that he was "using" the Christians to get votes. Well, they were having one of those telethons over it. Various people were asked to come on the program and say what they thought, so they called me up in Pasadena, where I was living then, and asked me to say a few words. When I walked into the studio that night you could have cut the tension in the air with a dull knife! His enemies were there kickin' a loser. You could just feel that they wanted to stomp him, maul him.

Mr. Nixon was sitting there on camera where they were asking the questions when I walked in and took my place. I looked at him a long time and I could see he was uptight. I felt for him so much

I just had to say something to try to relax him a little. So I kind of chuckled and said, "Well, one thing, you got a better make-up man now. You've got a friend in the make-up room!" He smiled, and it made me feel better for him. When it came my turn to speak my piece, I said, "I'm on here for just one purpose—to say that you, Mr. Nixon, did come on the Graham Crusade in nineteen fifty-seven. But I know your Christian background. You came to the Crusade because you were doing what comes naturally." That tired, tense man just sat back and grinned. That was when I first called him Dickie Boy, which broke up the whole TV studio audience! A good laugh will knock down more barriers than anything else sometimes. When I walked away from the cameras, it was almost like a celebration—everybody was huggin' and kissin' me. Everybody, that is, who was so concerned about how hurt he was from the awful slings and arrows they'd been shooting at him in that particular campaign.

I thought back on all this when I was dressing to go downstairs at the hotel in Washington, D.C. that January day in 1971, to sing at the White House Worship Service. Richard Nixon was no longer a wounded, defeated man. He was President of the United States. Dickie Boy and Patty Girl and Tricia and Julie were America's First Family and I was going to see them all again. I was honored and happy, looking forward to the whole thing.

Tedd Smith had come to play for me and I was to meet him and his wife, Thelma, downstairs outside the hotel lobby where the White House limousine would pick us up. Of course, everything at the White House is—*protocol*. Pro-to-col! You do every little thing according to what you're supposed to do. It's downright regimental. Protocol starts even before you get there. It's even "according to protocol" in the car going over. Bear this in mind, as I'm down at the entrance of the hotel with Tedd and Thelma. Pulled up by the curb was not one big, black official limousine, but two. You see, the minister of the East Whittier Friends Church in Whittier, California, the Rev. T. Eugene Coffin, was to be the speaker at the service. I used to know the Nixons' Quaker minister, the Rev. Ezra Stone, years before, but I'd only met this gentleman and his wife and when I found that protocol had it that I was to ride in the first car with them, while Tedd and Thelma Smith would come along in the second car, I thought I'd just go with Tedd where I felt more at home. So I piped up with, "If it's all right, I'll ride back here with Tedd and Thelma." Of course, nobody could do anything but agree, so I went on to say, "Since I don't fit comfortably in the rear seat because I have to back in, I'll just sit up front with the driver." I wasn't trying to be funny. It's true that when I get into these big, luxurious cars, I do have to back in because I just don't bend good.

We rolled up to the White House gate where the inspector or guard stands there with his book, checking. The first car, where I was *supposed* to be, rolled in but I wasn't there. We could all see the look of dismay on the inspector's face and I never saw anybody struggle not to break up the way our colored driver did. He was trying not to show it, but that man was having a ball! So was I. Then it was our turn to roll up to the gate and up we rolled—Tedd and Thelma in the back seat and me up front with the chauffeur! Oh, dear Jesus, I'm still *laughing*. The very conscientious inspector peered into the car, looked up and down his book, turned the pages . . . stooping down to look in the back of the car . . . then at me in the front. "Mr. Tedd Smith?" Tedd nodded. "Mrs. Tedd Smith?" Thelma nodded. Then I said, "Miss Ethel Waters." Well, he stared at me sitting up front and kept turning those pages, his face getting redder and redder.

Finally, I said, "I'm singing at the service this morning. I'm Miss Ethel Waters." His mouth flew open and he just stood there gaping at me. You see? He expected more pomp and circumstance. He had an *image*. Not only was my name down in his book for the front car, protocol had taught the fellow to expect me in the front car, with the others riding behind. He expected Miss Waters to come in as *he* expected her to come in! And here he finds this gray-haired woman laughing and talking with the driver on the *front* seat of the *second* car. I wish you could have seen that man trying to be dignified, trying to hold up his end of the protocol. He stood there for a minute, still flipping those pages and stuttering, "I'm—I'm trying to find the name. I'm—looking for the name." I said it had to be there because I was singing at the White House that morning. I didn't want us to be late, so I ended up telling him to look on his list for the first car. He found me listed and all in order, except in the wrong limousine and on the wrong seat. When we finally got past, the chauffeur was still trying to keep a straight protocol face, and I explained to him and the Smiths that I was sorry I hadn't put on some furs so I'd look more like Raquel Welch. I thought Tedd would fall off on the floor, he laughed so hard, and when he caught his breath, all he could say was, "Aw, Ethel, you're too much!"

So we got out of the car and went formally and sedately inside the mausoleum. That's what I said, the *mausoleum*—because that house is "white" and shining on the outside only. Inside, it's as cold and stiff as any mausoleum. They directed us to the East or West Room or whatever it was, and in spite of the formality, there I was smiling and saying "Hi" to everybody, but only me. Everybody else was standing straight and stiff like they might crack if they grinned—doing what they were supposed to do—according to protocol. I'm telling you, the atmosphere in that place was as unbending as at Buckingham Palace. But there we were, all standing around under those big portraits hanging over us on the walls— the Hall of Fame or Infamy—every painted face in every portrait looking down on you to see if you were about to make a mistake in protocol. Man, those pictures looked almost alive!

But when we were properly conducted into the room where the President and Patty Girl and all were waiting for us, things got, by comparison at least, so much nicer and friendlier, we almost forgot to go downstairs to have the meeting. After awhile, the phone rang to remind us we were due downstairs in the East Room, so we trooped down—sedate again, according to protocol—and set up all around the room, I saw those little gold chairs and got nervous about how frail and tiny they looked till I glanced at the platform and saw a row of heavier chairs for those who were to take part in the service. To myself I said, "Look, you won't have to try one of them little gold things—good."

They held back those of us who would participate until the others had settled onto those flimsy gold chairs, everybody prim and proper in rows, sitting up so precise, nobody even whispering. It was all so muted as we waited to go down the aisle to the platform, the President and the Quaker minister and Tedd and me, that when we finally started out, we kinda tipped in. So I could steady myself on his arm as I walked, I was being supported by a wonderful-looking young military officer and I nearly ruined him as we tipped along in that stiff silence by humming "Here Comes the Bride" under my breath. That boy had a time trying to keep a straight face and a military bearing. It was beautiful! I thought sure before he got me up there he'd flip.

Well, with my escort's help, I managed to get up on the platform and seated, but the whole place and everybody in it was so uncomfortable and subdued, I was almost afraid to arrange myself on my chair for fear I'd squeak. I did get fixed, though, and then I said to myself, "Dear God, this ain't no wake—this is a church meeting! These folks all look so miserable and we've come here to worship You!" I'm telling you the truth, I could almost hear them saying to themselves, "What am I doing in this cold place? Why in the world did I let myself get hooked into attending?"

There I was, sitting on my platform chair, still trying to smile a smile out of somebody out front. Do you think one single face cracked? No. I watched them, and the longer the organist played, the stiffer they all got because even the music was like a funeral. The whole thing was so sad, it still makes me yell and laugh to remember those first few minutes. I was determined the mausoleum and the protocol wouldn't get to me, and so I just sat there feeling the way I felt—exuberant. I couldn't see why the solemnity. I was effervescent. Jesus was there and I was going to sing three songs about Him, and so I went on smiling at those poor people with the long, solemn faces. Faces interest me. I like to study them. I kept spotting this one and that one, saying to myself how sure I was that he or she wished they'd been anywhere else on earth but there. You could tell just by looking which of the others were thinking how much all the sad, dutiful, enforced worship—with protocol—was bugging them.

The President made some nice, subdued opening remarks, introduced me, then Tedd, and explained that at certain places on the program I would sing my numbers. I looked at Tedd and he seemed to have the situation in hand, so I figured I'd just relax and go on studying the faces of those poor people. President Nixon made a few more quiet, polite comments and sat down. He then nodded to Tedd, and then Tedd nodded. I wasn't going to let them outdo me, so I nodded too. It seemed like it would be all right if I got up to be sure the mike was in the right place for me. The President nodded at me, I nodded at him, moved the mike around a little, and after another nod from the President, I knew it was time for me to sing my first number.

Well, I stood there a second, looking around at those three-hundred-and-some stiff, protocol-encrusted people and I said, "Now, you know I have a way of speaking when I'm at the Crusades. I only have one way of speaking anywhere, but *this* lets me know I'm at home with my family regardless. Regardless of where I am I've got to be at home with my children, so when I say this one word, if I get a certain response, then I know I'm with my family and that I'm welcome." I waited about two beats and shouted, "Hi!"

I waited again and there came back a slightly sick, anemic sound—something like "Hi." I knew I was crackin' protocol, but I couldn't help it. This time I broke out laughing and shouted, "*Hi!*" There wasn't anymore silence in the mausoleum. They brought down the place shouting "Hi!" back at me. From that minute, everybody relaxed. I sang my own song, "Partners with God," the Rev. Mr. Coffin prayed, I sang again, he preached, I sang my last number—"His Eye Is on the Sparrow"—the minister pronounced the benediction, the organist pronounced the Postlude, and we all went up to the reception room and I tell you, it was just beautiful!

You'd have thought it was a meeting of old friends. There was not one word of politics, no more stiff standing around wondering how to get out, there was just good, happy talk. It was beautiful! Everybody was shaking my hand, and instead of sour looks, they were all laughing and chatting with each other. The ice had thawed from the walls and all of us, including the President, had fun.

Even though I've been back to the White House since for Tricia's wedding, I still haven't had a chance to tell either the President or his wife about me switching limousines and causing that poor inspector at the gate to have a case of apoplexy. Maybe they'll read about it in this book. One thing I know, they'll laugh too!

Sometimes I have to stop and pinch myself to believe all the wonderful things my Lord has allowed to happen to me already in the 1970's. To me, it's wonderful! I needed the good fee I was paid to star in *Member* at the Ivanhoe in Chicago at the start of the decade because I knew I had to move into the nice place I live now, but even more than that, it just plain did me good to know I could still handle the heavy role of Berenice Sadie Brown in my present physical condition. Nineteen seventy-one began with the President inviting me to sing at the White House . . . then in the spring my child, Billy Graham, wanting me to be with him at his Award Dinner given by the National Conference of Christians and Jews . . . and in June of the same year, here comes my personal invitation to attend, along with only 399 other invited guests, the wedding of Tricia Nixon to Edward Finch Cox. The handsome, engraved invitation came just when my two children, Joyce Blackburn and Genie Price, arrived in Los Angeles to help me with this book. I took them into my bedroom and asked their advice in deciding which dress would be appropriate for such an important occasion.

We selected one we all thought would be fine, and I felt mighty relieved not to have to spend the money on a new dress. Still, after we finished our work and they had gone home, I got to thinking and stewing about that dress. Of course, Twila Knaack already had my plane reservations made, as always, and Bill and Joan Brown had sent my wedding gift on ahead, but since I was scheduled to sing at Billy's big Chicago Crusade the week of the wedding, I'd sent something on ahead too—a phone call to a dear girl in Chicago named Georgianna Jordan, a wonderful dress designer. Georgie is a skilled, professional designer, who makes costumes and dresses for weddings and other big, important functions. I love her dearly. She's a lovely Italian girl, who's known me from the professional world for years. We're just as close now as we were then. You don't change when the love of God's in your heart. You just go right on loving each other. Why, if I'd call Georgie tomorrow, she'd do all she could to help me out in whatever I needed. The Lord has people all around to take care of His children—I know. He has children everywhere to take care of—I almost called myself "this old buzzard," but no more! I'm a child of the King. So, although Georgie is no longer in the theater, but has gone into designing, nothing has changed between us. She seemed glad to hear my voice when I called her to swear her to secrecy about my concern over having just the right dress for the White House wedding. I told her I'd picked out a dress I already had that ought to be all right, but she caught right away how much that invitation meant to me and said she'd dream up just the right outfit by the time I got there. She acted so happy to be helping me with my secret project, I went farther out into orbit. Knowing I'm going to get to sing with Billy at a Crusade puts me into orbit too. It always has, but here were both wonderful events up ahead of me. And in the same week!

"Make it sensible, now, Georgie," I cautioned her. "You know my condition. Something might happen I can't even go to the wedding, but if you make it sensible, I'll have the dress for the Crusades anyway."

I got to Chicago on Thursday of the preceding week in order to rest from the long trip before the Crusade began, and I hadn't been in my room at the Holiday Inn on Lake Shore Drive any time at all, when I discovered that some of my Crusade children, bless their hearts, were already thinking about what Mom was going to wear! They wanted me to look just right.

Nobody pressured me that first day, though, and on Friday, Georgianna Jordan arrived to show me her sketch of this wonderful ensemble. Right off, I could see that what she had drawn was more to the point than what I'd brought along from my own closet. Georgie's outfit would be fine whether the wedding was held indoors in the White House or outside in the Rose Garden. Who could tell what the weather was going to be like? I told her I loved the dress and then, most tactfully (Georgie calls everybody darling or dear), she said, "Darling, what accessories did you bring with you? What do you have to go with this?" I showed her a hat I'd brought which I didn't like, and I showed her another affair I'd brought too—one of the little "envelopes" I usually wear at the Crusades.

"It fits well on my head," I told her, "and even though it's giving away a family secret, Georgie, I'll be frank with you, my hair grows extremely long—almost to my waist—I'm constantly having to keep trimming it off, but I'm bald on top!"

We had a good laugh over that and I explained that all those years I'd used hairpins up there to pin my braids around, I'd gouged the hair all out so it won't hold anymore. Georgie looked at the top of my head and caught on right away this was why I wear those handkerchief things that match my dresses and sort of dress up the mug. They look cute. Even a "hankerchief head" can look presentable if the handkerchief matches and is put on right. So to go by, Georgie took this one I'd brought, and if you saw me on

TV at the wedding, you know the one she made to match my dress turned out beautiful.

Right after Georgie left to shop for the material for my new ensemble, I got a phone call from Millie Dienert. Nearly everybody in the Crusade that week had been wondering what I'd wear! Those wonderful children had made some plans on their own. Millie told me that she and her husband, Fred, and Walter Bennett had already decided to make me a present of a new outfit because they were proud that I was going and really wanted me to look sharp. She'd called to find out if I felt up to going with her to the store right then to shop around. I thanked her and blessed her and Fred and Walter, but I had to tell her I'd already got the ball rolling with Georgie. I did say, "Millie, I want you to be sure to come by my room and look it over, when Georgie brings it. I want your candid opinion. Just as soon as the dress is here and on me, I'll call you."

The next day, here came Georgie for the fitting, and the big deal of getting me all together began. After she had pinned and tucked and fixed and I was resting in a comfortable chair, I got up enough courage to ask, "Now, what about shoes and my other accessories, Georgie?" I showed her the shoes I'd brought with me, which happened to be fifty-five-dollar shoes that hurt my feet terrible. I tell you, those tan shoes killed me! I was laughing, but by then, the whole thing was about to get me down.

Gentle-mannered Georgie, in her sweet way, looked at the shoes and then said, "Well, darling, I'll tell you . . ."

"I don't want to buy a new purse and I don't want to buy new shoes. These things hurt my feet, but I'm just not going to buy another pair of white shoes to wear to this wedding! After all, I'm *not* a 'member of the wedding,' I'm just a guest!" I got to laughing so hard, I began to cough. "Oh, dear Jesus, I've been in shock ever since I was invited to this thing, Georgie. It's putting me in the sanitarium! I want to go and I loved being asked, but I'll have to go somewhere afterward and take a vacation."

A recent picture of Miss Waters. *Faingold Studios.*

Tedd Smith, Miss Waters, and Don Hustad before a Crusade appearance.
*Billy Graham Evangelistic Association (Åke Lundberg Photo)*

President Richard Nixon greets the guest soloist at the White House Worship Service. *Billy Graham Evangelistic Association (Russ Busby Photo)*

With Reginald Beane.

With Grady Wilson.

Cliff Barrows introduces Miss Waters. *Billy Graham Evangelistic Association* (*Russ Busby Photo*)

Miss Waters at a Billy Graham Crusade. *Billy Graham Evangelistic Association* (*Åke Lundberg Photo*)

Miss Waters with Billy Graham. *Billy Graham Evangelistic Association (Russ Busby Photo)*

Billy Graham, George Beverly Shea, and Miss Waters singing a Crusade hymn. *Billy Graham Evangelistic Association (Russ Busby Photo)*

*Billy Graham Evangelistic Association (Russ Busby Photo)*

Georgie was still studying those hateful tan shoes and the (I thought) beautiful purse with gold trimming I'd brought along, hoping to carry.

"Well, dearie," she said at last, "I have a bag . . . I'll bring it tomorrow and let you see it. It's good-looking . . ."

"But you know I have things to *carry* in my purse. Can I get anything in yours?"

I could tell she was trying to keep me from getting too worked up. "I'll bring it. I'm sure it will look much better, and if you don't like it, darling . . ."

So here we come to the shoes again. I knew she wasn't going to let me get by with those shoes. She hadn't taken her eyes off them.

"The shoes might be all right, dear. Maybe they'll work with a touch of tan somewhere in your ensemble . . ."

That night I prayed, "Lord Jesus, help me get myself together for this wedding without comin' apart in the process!"

The next afternoon, when Georgie brought the dress, she also brought her purse, which she just laid down without a word and oh, I loved the outfit. It was stunning! That blessed child had pushed it to completion in jig time and the little toquelike thing she'd copied for my head was perfect. She'd given so much time to my dress, she didn't even bring up the small purse, just left it, hugged me, and hurried out the door.

Right away, while I still had the dress on, I phoned Millie Dienart to come on up to my room. I really wanted her to give her approval because Millie's a connoisseur of clothes. Well, I could tell by the look on her face before I ever asked, "How does this strike you? Will I look all right?"

"It's lovely, Mom! Really lovely. You'll be more than all right."

Then I said, "Millie, here's two pocketbooks." I showed her mine first, then Georgie's little one.

She compared. "The white one, the small one. It goes with your outfit."

*Billy Graham Evangelistic Association (Russ Busby Photo).*

I didn't argue. "Now, here's my shoes."

She hesitated, so I said, "Millie, you know me. Why can't I wear these shoes?"

Millie Dienert's like a little doll and I could tell she didn't want me to get any more upset either. "Let's think about gloves first. Do you have a pair of white gloves?"

"I sure do," I said proudly, pretty certain I'd score on the brand new pair of pure white gloves another precious child named Nancy Wolcott had given me when she came all the way from Lincoln, Illinois, to the Crusade that week. She had not only given me the gloves, she'd loaned me her own clip or whatever you call it that fastens to your purse to keep your gloves attached. I didn't know they had a thing like that. I wear my gloves in my pocketbook because my fingers swell, so that, like with rings, half the time I can hardly get them off once they're on my hands.

Up to that point, Millie seemed perfectly satisfied. I had my dress, my little hat, my gloves, Nancy's glove clip, Georgie's pocketbook . . . That left only the shoes. Oh, those tan shoes!

Millie was staring at them, frowning. I knew I was in for it.

"My mother has trouble with her feet too, Mom," she said carefully. "I've seen you in those shoes before and you were miserable. I won't let you go to the wedding with your feet hurting. Let's go get you a pair of the kind Mother thinks are so comfortable."

She went on to tell me about Neutralizers or Naturalizers, and still speaking very softly so as to keep me calm, she tried to persuade me.

"Millie, I have a bunion and it's sore. And my feet swell—and when they swell I almost have to cut my shoes off. I get water-logged, girl. Especially when I have to stand, my feet murder me. The brand is not the point. *My feet* are the point."

I wasn't inventing a bunion to keep from going out to shop that day. I admit I was tired from all the hullabaloo, but the problem I have with my feet swelling is no lie. It's just something I don't discuss or let show. Why, I can be out in public in that special kind of agony when your feet swell and you've got a sore bunion and a sore corn—standing there in absolute misery—and somebody will walk up and say, "Oh, Ethel, you look beautiful!" I could scream.

Millie paid me no mind. "I'm going to call up the store that carries Naturalizers and check anyway."

She used my phone and sure enough there was a store in Chicago that had my size, and before I could fuss anymore, Millie had me headed for this store.

Bless her heart, she had that shoe salesman bringing out every pair of Naturalizers my size in the place. He tried and he tried until the right pair turned up. I'd explained about the condition which caused my feet to swell and he got the message exactly. Even after he found a pair that felt good, he stretched one to fit over my bunion and the other to fit over my corn. "You've got the smallest feet, Miss Waters, considering this physical condition, and the narrowest heels!" Of course, I not only liked the shoes, I liked the man too. Since shopping is so difficult for me and since my feet have hurt me for so long, I decided to get two more pairs. Consequently, I've got three pairs of shoes that don't hurt and I'm glad.

Back at my room in the Holiday Inn, Millie and I decided I could tint my new white shoes after the wedding was over. I was stretched out on the bed, resting. Millie stayed with me awhile and was in the chair across the room. Neither of us had said anything for a few minutes, but it was all circling around in my mind still. I went over every item in my wedding outfit—dress, hat, gloves, purse, shoes —they all seemed to be there, ready for the big day. I was tired, but still so happy to be going to Washington. Only one thing bugged me. I just had to ask Millie one question: "Why does everybody ignore *my* pocketbook?"

"No one's ignoring it, Mom. It's a beautiful purse."

"Then why do I have to carry that little squinchy one? Little purses make me feel so big."

Millie smiled at me and said in her endearing way, "Well, they just aren't carrying big bags these days to an occasion like this wedding will be. It's just not *the* thing, Mom."

I was sure Millie knew, so I said, "All right. I can accept that." So I didn't carry mine. I carried Georgie's.

When I arrived at the Hotel Madison in Washington, there waiting for me was that precious, darling girl, Ruthie Graham. Tedd Smith's wife, Thelma, had told her about when she'd have me there from the airport, and I'd no sooner got in my room (next door to the Grahams') when Ruth called and invited me to have dinner with her in her room. I hope I didn't hug her too hard, but I was so glad to see her! She looked radiant. She was wearing a gift from Billy . . . a beautiful, flowing peignoir. I tried to tell her how lovely she looked. We ordered dinner in her room and I enjoyed every bite and every word of conversation. This was the first time I'd told the story of all that went on getting Mom Waters together for the wedding, and her sense of humor egged me on. We both laughed like we needed it, and I don't know anybody who doesn't.

She'd told me Billy wouldn't get in till the wee small hours, since the Chicago Crusade was still going on and he had to preach Friday night and couldn't catch an earlier plane. I told her to try to get some rest while she waited for him. We said good-night, and I promised I'd call their room at nine in the morning.

I guess I slept some, but my heart was pounding from the excitement and anticipation of Saturday and the wedding. In the morning I rang Ruthie on the phone, and the first thing she wanted to know was if I'd had breakfast yet. Billy wanted me to join them. I had, and told her to thank Billy anyway, but I thought I'd better rest until time to head for the White House and besides, those two needed to be by themselves.

She gave me a good report of the Crusade meeting the night before, said Billy didn't get in till 3:00 A.M., but had slept well the few hours he had left. We made our plans where we would meet, since I was to go to the wedding with them, but before I hung up I said, "Ruth, I paid good money for this coat I brought along, but with all that hot weather out there do you think it's all right if I don't wear it? I want to look right, and my coat's just beautiful, but Washington, D.C. can be the hottest place this side of the other one and my pocketbook's too small to carry a wad of Kleenex in and I know I'm going to sweat all over the place!" By now Ruthie was laughing, I kept on complaining, because she was turning around to tell Billy about my fussin' and fumin'—and I was purposely keeping them in stitches. "I'll have to carry my Kleenex in my hand. I forgot to put in even one handkerchief— and I've got some *gorgeous* ones." That's true. I own some price-less handkerchiefs and at the wedding of the daughter of the President of the United States, I had to carry Kleenex in my hand!

Around a quarter to three, the limousine came for us and it had started to drizzle. Just as we got out of the car, more than a drizzle was coming down. There I was, of course, without my coat, so Billy threw his around me—only it wasn't his. It was Grady's raincoat and it pretty well hid the outfit Georgie had designed for me! There we went, the three of us, sashayin' up the walk to the White House.

Now, I want to say something here from my heart. That was the closest I'd ever felt to Billy and Ruth. The talk Ruthie and I had the night before was beautiful, but walking into the White House between those two precious people was like a long-time dream come true for me. President Nixon was no more proud as he walked with Tricia that day than I was to be going along between Billy and Ruth. They were like my own children to me as I went with them up those stairs to that wedding. I felt like a million dollars with my babies. Just like Richard Nixon felt with his daughter on his arm, that's how I felt with my son and daughter. That's true. That's really true.

Some mail had been forwarded to me from Los Angeles to Chi-cago and in it must have been the pass I needed to get in, but me being so excited or looking for something else in the pile, I was careless and overlooked and when I got to the White House at last, after *all that preparation*, suddenly I realized I didn't have my pass card!

Billy said, "Where's your pass, Ethel?"

I looked straight ahead and answered, "It must have come after I left Chicago." Oh, I'm still laughing. But fortunately, the young man with the list this time wasn't as flustered as the inspector at the gate had been the day I was riding in the wrong car. He calmly read his list and there was Ethel Waters' name and address in black and white—or I just wouldn't have got in! When I flew back to Chicago, I found that thing. It had come before I left, all right, but the Devil had buried it under the other mail!

Well, we got in and naturally people began right off conferring with Billy, but Ruth, knowing how shaky I am, stayed close by me in the crowd. She knows I need to touch her arm to steady myself and keep my sense of security. I hope it looks like I am kind of sauntering along, speaking to this one and that. To some it might seem I'm overfriendly with Ruth and others, but touching someone's arm is a protection method I use so it doesn't show too much that I can't hurry when I walk or don't have good balance anymore.

Ruth and I, with Billy close by talking to people, got into this room where guests were congregating. I took in the picture in quick order. Sitting on a couch like the Culhanes were three "types"— two women and a man. When I walked in, right off I spotted that "look" on their faces—that "look" the same as said, "What's *she* doing here?" Oh, boy! I whispered to Ruth, "Uh, oh." She smiled very sweetly at me and said in a courteous voice, "Sit down here, Ethel," pointing at the sofa where the *three* were parked. "I know you need to sit down." I did, because it was quite a walk up those stairs and around, but you had to take that walk to pass the cameras. I would gladly have made a short cut behind the bushes just to get in, I was already so tired, but they wanted me to pass the TV cameras. Do you get the picture? I did need to sit down and the first available place was on that sofa. There was plenty of room. The couch was king size. Well, the three "occupants" *froze* when I sat down. They froze and I tried to shrink so I couldn't touch them. I wasn't laughing then, but it was hard not to. I looked up at Ruth and indicated that there was space for her to sit there too, but she said she'd stand, and poor Billy had to stand from the time he got there till the time he left except during the wedding.

I sat by the "three" on the sofa as people kept coming by to greet me. Pretty soon another lady came over (from an eye signal, I gathered she knew *them* and they her) to speak to my seatmates. Finally she got to me and said very politely, "Oh, Miss Waters, I've always admired you!" The "three" hadn't so much as nodded in my direction, and I sat there all shrunk up as best I could with so many people coming up to speak to me. The lady who said she'd always admired me, smiled at me and asked, "Uh—which side are you with, Miss Waters? Was your invitation from the Nixons or the Coxes?"

"I'm with the Nixons," I answered. It was all I could do to keep from laughing! My couchmates now understood what *I* was doing there.

When we started assembling to go out to the wedding we had to stand and stand and stand, because the rain played little tricks, and all that standing began to take its toll on me. There was lightning, then the rain would come down and then it would let up. Finally, the President said the wedding was going to be in the garden whether the rain stopped or not. That settled it and we began to move slowly out again, but people got all jammed up in the gallery part in the lower hall and it was so hot and muggy, I started to feel a little woozy wedged in with all those people. But there we stood.

I've got a way of looking things over when I don't seem to be paying any attention. Even when I'm getting awfully tired, as I was by then. I'd spotted an ordinary-looking chap in the crowd, and every time I turned to glance at him, he was sauntering slowly back and forth near Billy. I thought to myself, this bird ain't dressed for the occasion, what's *he* doing here? My suspicion and my set opinion was that the man was up to no good. (That Devil!) I was watching the man and he seemed to be watching me. I was *sure* he was trying to overhear something, because Billy was in deep, animated conversation. Finally I whispered to Ruth, "Don't look now, but that bird's been hoverin'. I imagine he has somethin' hidden in his pocket to take down whatever Billy's saying! But he'll not get any closer to Billy. He won't get by me—I'll block him!" Of course, I realize now, it was probably a security man protecting Billy. Wouldn't that have been something if I'd blocked him?

A few minutes later, for sure I pulled a social boo-boo when I spotted J. Edgar Hoover, moving toward me in the crowd. I yelled, "*Hello,* Mr. Hoover—how are *you?*" And when he reached for my hands, I gave him a big bear hug! He seemed *so happy* to see a friendly face. I like the man and I'd have hugged him if I'd had to break ranks to do it! Next in the crowd, I looked up and saw my darling Red Skelton and I hugged him too. When I feel that way about people, I just go ahead and show it. I want them to know I like them. I admire Red Skelton. We worked together on the same bill years ago, and he is a genius if there ever was one. So many entertainers right now pattern off of the routines that man has created out of his God-given ability. I just plain like Red Skelton. I just plain like J. Edgar Hoover. Years ago I sent Mr. Hoover my record albums, and he sent me a book with a lovely autograph. You know, public figures can be so different from the way they're depicted. If you know them personally, and you think they're genuine, nine times out of ten they'll feel the same about you. If you're phony, you're going to see phoniness in other people, but if you're real and not closed up, you're going to look for reality and detect it too, in the other person, no matter what people say about them. All of us make big mistakes in our thinking about people we don't know firsthand.

When we finally made it outside to the garden, there was a lot more breathing and walking space and oh, it was ethereally beautiful! Nothing, nothing can compete with or overshadow God's natural beauty, but in that garden man's beauty blended with God's overwhelming beauty and the rain had made it all just right. It was still and fresh, filled with peace and love. If you ask me how I'd describe it, I'd have to say that right there in the midst of the capital city of the greatest country on earth, the atmosphere was somehow exquisitely pastoral, as though the city had fallen back, so that only the gentle quiet of a country garden was there.

To me, the wedding ceremony was to the point—simple and full of meaning. Everything was just right, picturesque, like a fairy-land and yet all real. I was so happy to be there in all that beauty, so full of joy to be with Billy and Ruth, I don't recall too much about the music, except it was refreshing, like the rain, and you didn't have to walk in step with that old *dum-dum-te-dum, dum-dum-te-dum* thing. The whole ceremony was perfectly timed, without rush, and nothing interfered, nothing broke the spell. I was thankful it wasn't held in the house simply because I think walls harbor tension and tragedy and bad feelings and everything else. Out there in the garden, there was nothing but peace and harmony and love. Inside that White House? Wow! Even the portraits speak—some glower—and you wonder and shudder over when John Doe was President. There are many things—reminders, memories—inside that place to take your mind off what we were there for. In the garden, nothing distracted. It didn't even sprinkle again until after, and those seats weren't wet—for *me*. I'm giving you only one woman's opinion there. Maybe my fat didn't let me feel those "soggy cushions." Could be.

I knew my child Billy had to leave right away, to fly back to Chicago in time to make that night's service. I was concerned about him being so tired. More concerned than I might have been, I guess, if all of a sudden I hadn't run out of steam myself. I shouldn't have worried about him, and I asked the Lord to forgive me because I knew He wasn't about to make any mistakes. But when I saw Billy leave, I was ready to leave too. I was flying back to Chicago myself the next day to sing at the closing service of the Crusade. But after we said good-by to Billy, it was suddenly one of those things—mission accomplished.

I stood in the garden after he'd gone and was so thankful to my Lord that He had given me the physical strength and energy to be there, but this real tiredness had come over me. Ruth could see out of the corner of her eye that I was beginning to sag. So, when the President and the First Lady sent special word that they wanted Ruthie and me to come to visit with them in their library, I saw her shake her head. To accept their gracious invitation, it meant we would have had to go back the same long way, past those cameras, a long, long way to me at that point. I knew I was beginning to lean more heavily on Ruth. I could feel my body was beginning to swell from the heat and being packed in that crowd so long.

We had to go back to that same gallery where we'd got so jammed up before the wedding, no matter what, but as the guests were enjoying their champagne and laughing and chatting about the lovely ceremony, I said I just had to sit down somewhere. Only then did I realize I hadn't had anything in my stomach all day but a cup of coffee and two pieces of toast. That's all I'd eaten because I didn't know what the repast at the wedding was going to be and I'd taken these strong pills I have to take all the time.

I guess I looked done in, because the President's great friend, Charles "Bebe" Rebozo, saw me sitting there and came over to me. People were still coming up to talk to me, but I know Mr. Rebozo could tell by my watery eyes and the thickness in my speech that the fire was out. Certainly Ruth knew I'd made all the effort I could make, so she whispered, "I'm going to take you home—get you back to our hotel." She knows that when I pass out from exhaustion, it happens just like that. I'm gone. So she explained to Mr. Rebozo and asked him to make it clear to President and Mrs. Nixon why we couldn't accept their kind invitation to the family get-together.

On our way out, one of the President's aides came running up
and said the President was expecting us in the library. What the
President didn't know was that I couldn't have made it to the
library. I was well aware that the Nixons could not show any
favoritism toward me or anyone. These days you can't show any
preference to people age-wise, profession-wise, or anything else
without somebody getting offended. Even if I'd been carried in
on a stretcher, President Nixon couldn't have seen me unless I
waited my turn. I didn't have the strength for that. I don't have
the same protection from people that he has. People can get to me,
and with love they can overcome me. With all good intention,
they can just talk to me or pet me and before you know it, I could
have a heart attack on the spot. I try to avoid being overwhelmed
by people above everything else, especially when I'm tired already.
I tend to keep giving and giving, but I try to know when to stop. I
was invited to the wedding and to the family gathering afterwards,
but the thing I want to get across is this—if the Nixons *hadn't*
asked me, I'd have loved them just as dearly. I went because I
wanted so much to go. God gave me the strength and I loved every
minute of it, but the fire *was* out.

Once Mr. Rebozo promised to take my apologies to the President, I had no regrets when Ruth, who even in her sweet way can
be a little General, hurried me back to our hotel. I couldn't have
any regrets and I was ready to go. It had been too beautiful for an
anticlimax, for an encore of any kind.

# Part Six

There's still so much I don't understand about myself. I've been so sure about so many things and at the same time seem to understand myself so little. People put you down and people praise. It's hard to see yourself plain sometimes. Much of the time, for me. I am certainly more comfortable with Ethel Waters now that she is a Christian, but I don't understand her all the time.

People call me an artist, a great actress. I don't. I contend that I relive from my own experience in the roles I play. All of them. From comedy to tragedy. I've had my share of laughs, but I'm also a connoisseur of suffering and bitter experience. To relive in a part, as I do, costs. It costs me.

No one who hasn't done it can know what a strain it is to play a part like Berenice Sadie Brown in *The Member of the Wedding*. It isn't easy. It drains the very life out of me because I *live it*. I have to. Other actors may approach their parts in other ways, but aside from the fact that like everybody, I've got to memorize lines, I don't prepare in any other way.

You take that scene people still talk about from *Member* where I sit at the table as Berenice Sadie Brown, telling the children in the play, Frankie (Julie Harris) and John Henry (Brandon De Wilde), about the death of Ludie, the one man Berenice had ever loved. The one man who'd ever made Berenice Sadie Brown truly happy. The children keep asking Berenice questions, but her mind is way back to when Ludie died. She sits there at the kitchen table and *relives* her own agony. I still remember the lines:

[It was] The coldest November I ever seen. Every morning there was frost and puddles were crusted with ice. The sunshine was pale yellow like it is in winter time. Sounds carried far away, and I remember a hound dog that used to howl toward sundown. And everything I seen come to me as a kind of sign. . . . And it was a Thursday towards six o'clock. . . . I remember I went to the passage and opened the front door. Dark was coming on; the old hound was howling far away. And I go back in the room and lay down on Ludie's bed. I lay myself down over Ludie with my arms spread out and my face on his face. And I pray that the Lord would contage my strength to him. And I ask the Lord to let it be anybody, but not let it be Ludie. And I lay there and pray for a long time. Until night.

Ludie was dead. I was playing the woman who had loved him so dearly and who had tried to bring back his strength through her own. But to me, Ethel Waters, as I sat at that table through all those hundreds of performances on and off Broadway, it wasn't a man I grieved for. It was my own precious little grandmother, Sally Anderson, who died of cancer and I was with her. It was her death I *relived* on that stage. I remember her death as though it happened last night. When I got out to the place where she lived in the country, my grandmother's frail little body was still warm . . . but she was dead. There was a hole in her from the cancer. I must have been about fourteen years old and I loved her with all my heart, because she had always seemed to understand me. I picked that warm, dead small body up in my arms. The body had a funny odor. She was skin and bones, and although I was just a girl, I was holding her in my arms and trying to breathe my own *breath* into her mouth. Trying to put my own strength into her little old body. I tried, oh, how I *tried*. And when I played that scene at the kitchen table in *Member,* I wasn't talking about Ludie, a man. I was talking about Sally Anderson. That's why I say when people try to tell me I'm a great actress (though I appreciate their feelings)—I say, I've just got a good memory!

When people praise my "marvelous acting ability," they don't know that when I used to sing "Supper Time" in *As Thousands Cheer* and later in my one-woman shows, that again, I was reliving. This heart-rending song by Irving Berlin is the wail of a woman who, for the sake of her children, had to go on and try to fix supper—even though her man wouldn't be "comin' home no more." He had been lynched. I had not only spent time in the home of a Southern colored family whose beloved son had been lynched, so that I could relive the agony I'd shared with them. I was almost lynched once myself in Georgia a long time ago, by a theater operator who wanted me out of his way.

So I am humble and grateful for all the accolades and I have always tried to do my best, but more than acting, I have *relived*. Remembered. And I can't explain much more than that about myself as an artist. Seemingly, I was versatile enough to cover many angles of the profession. I did legit, movies, clubs, carnivals —I sang, I danced, I portrayed more roles than I can remember. In my young days, when it was popular, I was even famous for my shimmy! People would talk me into trying this or that—always something new—all things I was sure would flop. I'd be sure I'd flop in them, but I'd go ahead and do it to prove my point, and it would be sensational! But I wouldn't understand about how I brought it off. That's the way my salary took such leaps and bounds. I'd ask for the most scandalous amount of money (to me), being *sure* they would say No, but by gum swickety, I'd get it! Then I'd die ten thousand deaths, because I never felt sure I could bring it off at all.

And this is the truth, as I have to face my Maker, I never, *never* walked out onto a stage or anywhere to perform that I didn't first, quietly to myself, plead, "Oh, dear Lord, please let me earn my salary. Let me please the people. Help me do my best." I didn't cry out to God for His help because I was convinced that what I was going to do was the right thing. There's a narrow line here. I didn't call myself a Christian openly then. I didn't claim that what I was going to do would glorify God. I loved Him as much as I understood about Him and me. As I hearken back now in my old age, I try to understand lots of things about myself and I fail. But I know one thing: although I didn't know how, and I admit I didn't take any steps in His direction on my own until 1957, I always believed that one day I'd find my way back. I never lost touch with Him. I felt the Lord was displeased because I hated that girl who clawed my face. But I kept praying. I wanted Him to know I still loved Him, but you see, until I heard Billy preach, I thought (all through those years!) that I'd have to find a way to *prove* it to God.

When I'd come off the stage, I'd always say, "Oh thank You Lord for helping me please the people." In the main, I've always been applause *deaf*. It didn't thrill me. It simply reassured me. Anybody who was with me in the business through all those years can tell you that sometimes I'd be on the stairs or the elevator (if they had one) ready to dress and leave the theater, when I'd have to be called back to go out on the stage again and take bows. I always tried not to listen long to the applause, because when you depend on it, you're a dead duck! You know, there's such a thing as a golden silence . . . and when you get that golden silence, you know it's a real tribute. People have told me that they were too awed, too moved after some performance of mine, to do anything.

You can believe me or not, but I never understood that, either. I've just accepted it. I've just been thankful.

I liked beautiful clothes. I still do, but I can honestly say that I've been mostly satisfied with what I've had in my life. I came up having to be satisfied! Don't think I didn't appreciate the applause and *things* my money could buy. But whatever came, I tried just to be thankful.

People go around crying with a loaf of bread under their arm. Well, I've always been thankful for my loaf of bread. If it wasn't the kind of bread I wanted, I wouldn't let them sell me on some other kind, because *that* was the bread I had!

I never took nobody's job. When a director asked me to do a

part, I'd say, "Who are you dismissing to put me in?" It was hard to replace me, they always said, because I could fill in on any kind of job—if they had a gap, I'd fit into it. The material I had sometimes was *nothing*. But I knew so much about life—about joy and laughter and sorrow and tears and suffering—I wasn't one-tracked. I still go to the school of life, because experience is the best teacher. But before you can learn, even from *life,* you've got to admit that you need to learn. You've got to take up the lessons you've learned—good and bad—and make use of them. You've got to admit that you need to learn. So many people don't learn because they're too stupid to admit that they're dumb!

I'm still a thankful person, even though I've had to fight almost every inch of the way. Maybe that's one of the reasons I've been able to give thanks for that loaf of bread under my arm.

The Lord keeps me filled with awe—a-w-e. Like when that big earthquake hit Los Angeles early in 1971. I was all by myself, lying on my bed, and the building started swaying. I tell you, it *rocked.* And me right with it. I was literally "swingin' and sway-in'!" But He kept me from being frightened. I kept saying, "Speak, Lord, thy servant heareth. You know where I live, Jesus, and I got Your address too!"

We miss a lot in life because we don't know when to quit, what to leave out. Talented performers, writers, musicians, painters, anybody can ruin their work by going overboard. By never learning to be satisfied, by never knowing when to stop. The world is full of dissatisfied Christians too, because they're always straining at the bit to get more of some kind of feeling or experience when only Jesus Himself satisfies. There's a difference between the words *dis*satisfied and *un*satisfied. I desperately need more knowledge of my Lord, more understanding of His Word. *Un*satisfied is the way we ought to be. Hungry. But as I see it, no Christians need to be *dis*satisfied. I'll never be part of a fighting denomination because I'm just a born-again Christian, nothing more. We put too much emphasis on denominations and not enough on God Himself.

That's what I like about the Crusades and even the Sunday Worship Services at the White House where any and all denominations are welcome. I had to laugh to myself when I was at the White House at Tricia's wedding because everybody there seemed surprised at everybody else that was there—like they just didn't expect to see them. I guess it'll be the same way in heaven.

I'm censured sometimes because of my beliefs about denominations or lack of them. They're fine with me if they satisfy people. And I don't censure nobody for what they think. The only thing I object to is when they try to turn me around to their way of thinking when I'm satisfied with my own way. For example, some of the so-called "big names" in one denomination or another still call and ask me to sing for them. I can't do it because people at large would immediately think I'm connected with that faith or that emphasis. In the Graham Crusades, *only* Jesus Christ is preached. I'm at home singing there.

Once a kind, lovely man, a minister in one of these groups, wanted to know what I had against them. I said, *"Nothing."* Then he told me it hurt him that a fine Christian like me hadn't developed the "higher" something his group had. I calmly replied, "Well, it shouldn't hurt you. You've developed it and you enjoy it. I'm glad for you. Why can't you just be glad for me? *I enjoy what I've got with Jesus.* It would be different if I were dissatisfied, but I'm not. I'm not. I like what I've got. *I like it.*" In the Bible it says that if you believe on Jesus Christ, you have Eternal Life. I do, so I plan on going to heaven. I also plan on a lot of surprises there too!

But one person I won't be surprised to see again, because I know I will, is my mother Momweeze. I was never sure of her love when I was coming up, as a child, but I understood, when I got old enough, that the circumstances of my birth, which she hated, caused her not to love me as she might have. The reason she hated my illegitimate birth was because with what understanding she possessed, she *loved* Jesus. Momweeze died in the sixties, but although I grieved deeply because I had adored her all of my life, I was consoled and comforted, knowing I'd see her again in heaven where we would both be free to love each other enough to make up for all the years of my troubled childhood.

Even before I had rededicated my life to Jesus Christ in 1957, my mother and I had begun to be more reconciled. She seemed to accept me as her own at last, and even though she was a slow thinker at best, and ill much of the time, Momweeze began to encourage me and let me know she believed in Ethel, her daughter. In her later years, we came to a closeness and an understanding between us which I still cherish.

Because I traveled around so much, she lived in Philadelphia with my sister, Genevieve, but the last time I saw her, we really enjoyed being together. Momweeze seemed to feel pretty good, but not long after I had returned to California from that visit, I had a call from Genevieve, telling me that my mother was not doing so well. That she wasn't eating. I always sent money for her care and urged Genevieve to get her to a doctor. Right after that I received a call from a studio wanting me to make a quick movie at very good money. A short movie—no compromise—and I would have very few lines, but it was my name they wanted. I did the movie and decided I'd treat myself to a trip back to Philadelphia so I could see with my own eyes how Momweeze was doing. I also had two church programs scheduled. The one thing in my life that had come to be so important by then was to sing about my wonderful Saviour, but I planned to leave as soon as the programs were finished.

I did one of the church concerts, and before the second date had come up, Genevieve called again one morning to tell me Momweeze was worse and in the hospital. Her leg was infected and gangrene had set in. I told my sister I'd be there as soon as I did my one remaining date the next night. All the day of the concert I waited for a call, but none came, so I sang the program and was getting ready to fly East, when my telephone rang. It was

Genevieve. I said "Hello" and she said, "Well, she's dead. She's gone."

Momweeze had been unconscious, they had amputed her leg, but she never regained consciousness.

I hung up and sat there a long time, holding two very comforting thoughts. I knew that I had cared for her all through the years. She had never wanted for anything she needed. I gave her everything I could—and I loved her. The second comforting thought was that now I *knew* I'd see her again and she'd be all right.

I called a lady I know in Philadelphia and she took care of getting the remains from the hospital to the funeral home, and with the money I made on the movie, we buried her. There was no use in my going East. Momweeze was in heaven.

The night of her funeral, I had agreed to give a program for Youth for Christ. Don't forget, this was back in the sixties and I was still so sick from all that weight, my heart acted up something awful when I overdid. Thankfully, at this program my children, Dick Bolks and Paul DeKorte, were working with me. To help me out, they'd do a session of song between my numbers so I could have time to get my breath. Momweeze's favorite song had been "Just a Closer Walk with Thee." That night I managed the entire program of my numbers until I got to "Closer Walk," when I began to crack up. I finished it, but couldn't control my tears any longer. Dick said, "Why, Mom, what's the matter?"

I whispered, "They buried my mother today."

Momweeze is gone. There's only Genevieve left to me now. But I'll see Momweeze again. I'll see her someday. I don't have to worry about her anymore. She's with Jesus.

I do live, though, with a deep kind of helpless longing over some of my children I've known in the professional world. I love them and I sit here propped up in my bed at night and watch them on TV and long over them. Their talents are tops. I see them working there in those TV studios, or maybe I'm watching an old movie and one of my children is the star, or doing a top-notch piece of work as a supporting player, or is one of the fine comedians. They're entertaining the people, making them laugh or cry, but I see sadness and unhappiness in their precious faces, in their eyes. There are often tears in my eyes over them, three in particular, and I say to myself, oh, if I could only just get to you and talk to you—I know what you need, baby. But that "head-on" approach has been so abused, I'd never try it. I know what they'd say: "Oh, here *she* comes, and I like Ethel—I like Mom. I don't want to hurt her, but what'll I do?" They're scared! They're just plain *scared* of Christians. I know the children I'm talking about could get some sort of comfort from me. I don't mean cramming the Bible down their throats, because sometimes you can just gently talk to people without any Scripture and get a lot said. A lot that matters and comforts them. The Lord will give us the right things to say if He's in our hearts. To me, it's sad that people don't realize that. They go barging in and frighten needy people away from Jesus! Some of the biggest devils on earth are running around with Bibles in their hands. There ain't nobody can shove Jesus into a human heart. He waits. He waits until *He* knows that heart is open. I know from my own experience. You have to reach out for yourself. Oh, how I long to tell some of my children that if they would only just *go to Him*—not to a counselor, not to any other human being—just to Jesus. He's there. He's always ready. He's the One and He's been ready from the beginning to receive and forgive and love anybody, *anybody* who'll just be daring enough to claim Him. Some Christians scare these children, but thank God, Jesus isn't like that. He does the best He can to show His love, in spite of some of us Christians.

I watch these babies on TV and I think about them and talk to God about them, each one, and I long for the chance—a natural, down-to-earth chance just to talk to them—to tell them that I know. *I know.* That I once had that same unhappy look. I did, and I feel I could explain to them so they wouldn't be scared, about Jesus

and me *now*. I won't go at 'em, because of the reputation some
Christians have set up by hounding people. These children are
sensitive, they're tender underneath all that makeup. Their hearts
are broken, some of them, or heavy with burdens they can't carry.
None of this shows to most of the folks that watch their brilliant
performances, but Mom sees it and she grieves over them.

I ask God every day for His right time for me to have a chance
to tell them, before I go to heaven.

Of course, some of the people out there in my old world are
not sympathetic toward me because I follow my Lord now as best
I can. Some are glad for me. Some have told me they longed to
know the peace I enjoy. But others just don't understand. I don't
hold it against them for not understanding. They're in darkness,
most of them. I lived in disobedience to God for years, but I didn't
have the excuse of darkness. I had known Jesus Christ and His
love since I was twelve years old. Some of the people connected
with the Ivanhoe run of *Member* in Chicago in 1970 were furious
at me because I wouldn't agree to go on to Cleveland with the
package at a *fabulous* increase in pay, and I was making big money
on the Chicago run. Physically, I was just not able to continue,
and if I had, I'd have damaged my heart so that I would have put
myself out of commission to sing about Jesus at the Crusades.

I honestly feel I was to do that six-week stint in Chicago for a
reason. You see, in spite of all the money I've made down through
the years, I don't have any now. Just a very small nest egg to
depend on—what's left from the sale of my home on Hobart in
Los Angeles, and when it gets down to a certain level—it's like the
rain falling—God refills it and the level comes up, just enough.
I never know when I'll have to tap that reserve, but I don't worry.
Like it says in my song, "Partners with God." You don't need a
lot of money when He's in charge of your affairs. You need only
what you need. I'm not countin' on this book, but I have a feeling
that it may be the thing He'll use to prevent my little well from
going dry before it comes time for me to go to heaven to live with

Him. For the time being, that six weeks of singing "Sparrow" in *The Member of the Wedding* at the Ivanhoe raised the level back up in my well.

I long to be able to tell these children I grieve over that the world don't come to an end when you begin to follow Jesus. It just starts turning for you! He gives you the strength to do things you never thought you could do. He knows no two of us is alike. I've done what I believed He told me to do. He'll tell you too, in His own way, according to what He, your Creator, knows about *you*. He is far more original and creative than the most artistic person on earth. He didn't waste His time making *duplicates* of people.

Of course, once you've stepped into the circle of His wonderful love, the temptations will start. Oh, boy! But you know there's such a thing as the first day at the race track, the same as I know. That first day, you're a big winner. You keep on winning until you lose your shirt, but by then, you're hooked. That's the way it is when you turn to God. You get all kinds of juicy offers, but if your turning has been for real, you've got to refuse them. You'll know what in your life is *mammon* in God's eyes. And children, it's true, you just can't follow God *and* mammon. It's not that Jesus meant to be cruel when He said that. It's just that He knew it wouldn't work. It's too hard on any human to straddle like that. It tears you in two. And He wants you in one piece, strong, full of courage, able to love even those who despise you.

Don't you children ever believe that *anything* God demands of us will hurt us in the long run. I never drank in my life beyond my fifth year when, for kicks, I'd sample from one of my relatives' hidden bottles or swipe my mother's Lydia Pinkham. But as I grew up I began to hate liquor because of what it did to my two aunts. I soon learned that when they were sober they were my friends, but when they were drinking we lost our friendship and I became their victim.

When I began singing professionally, I didn't drink because I wanted to do my best. Every time I sang, I had to sell my *ability* and my talent. There was no song in my reportoire like "I'll get by as long as I have you" or anybody else. I just had my artistry. I didn't gamble, either. I was married to a gambling addict and I knew what excess of dope and drink or gambling or anything else could do. I'd paid off too many IOU's for other people. I'm not saying you'll have to do this or that. I never tried to tell other people how to live and I'm not about to. Like the saying goes, "A fool convinced against his will is of the same opinion still." If you children will just want to seek God yourselves, He'll help you overcome any real problems you have.

I'm a follower of Jesus Christ because I'm simply convinced that God and life go hand in hand. I'm convinced, too, that nobody—*nobody* knows how to live life at its fullest unless he or she walks minute by minute with our precious Lord.

I wasn't a goody person. I'm not that now. I just want to be His child. Maybe that's why I adore Paul in the Bible. Don't forget, before he was Paul, he was Saul. He didn't get his name or his heart changed except by Jesus. He was really just what he claimed to be, "the chiefest of sinners." Some of the worst of us make the happiest Christians. The further we've gone as sinners, the more enlightened believers we can become. If you don't know you've got a big, crying need as a sinner, the blessed Saviour can do nothing for you. But if you've got a deep need and you know it and you come to Him and want deliverance, oh boy! He can do it for you, whatever it is. He can do it. None of this is easy to believe except by faith, but who are we to doubt His power. It all depends on your *wanting* him by faith and in humble belief to completely give over your will to Him.

I do understand enough about myself to know that when I get to heaven, I'll be overjoyed just to stand in line, knowing at last I'm in His presence. His love does this to us. Love that is always giving. Oh, I just love Him. I love Him. How I *long* for you children to love Him too.

I have loved Jesus Christ all my life, but I think I had to surrender myself to Him before I knew how to love other people. In spite of all my success and all the happiness I tried to give to my audiences, there was no personal happiness in me. I was a high-strung person by nature, but thank heaven I'm under the control of my Saviour now. I had no real happiness then. I have it now with Jesus. And the happiness and peace I have, you can have. There's more than enough to go around. What I've got I don't take from nobody else. There's enough. I'm sorry I didn't have the understanding of God's forgiveness so I could forgive that girl who clawed my face back in the little colored church in Chester. I missed a lot of peace through the years, but I'm glad I didn't straddle the fence like a lot of Christians I know. I'm glad I didn't pretend there was no hate in my heart and become a hypocrite. I'm around church people a lot these days and you can always tell how much of their professing is real.

I'm still a nervous person. More so since I'm older and not well and I know I'm still misunderstood. Just the way my family never understood me, considered me sharp-tongued, hard to handle. *High strung*. But God knows what causes us to be that way. He knows the root of it. I comfort myself by remembering this when I'm in a Crusade crowd and people push up to get me to autograph this and that. It makes me *so nervous* when they do this, I think sometimes I'll pass right out. I'm grateful, oh, Lord, I'm grateful that they love me, that the public still wants to hear me perform, but I get a kind of claustrophobia when they crowd around me. I don't think a church or a Christian Crusade is the place for celebrity hunting and autograph signing anyway! But mainly these days I get confused, nervous, and jittery. I have a hard time writing because of my illness. Twila Knaack can tell you how easy it is for me to mess up an address. And I think my nervousness causes me to forget things. At least, it helps the Devil out when he tries to blank my memory. I hope a lot of older people whose bodies are wearing out the way mine is, will read this book so they won't think they're the only ones who get confused and mixed up under pressure. But I've stopped questioning these times. I've simplified it down to where I can handle each day as it comes, by facing the fact that *Jesus knows* what I need to remember and He won't let me forget the important things. It's very simple and I'm putting it this way because it is so simple, *if* you really believe Him.

I'm into my old age now, but I don't have anything special to say to older people any more than I have to young. People are people. The young have the handicap of no experience. The old have the handicap of infirmity, of weakened bodies, and sometimes they're confused in their minds. So are the young. What keeps me steady in my old age is what I've already told—closeness to Jesus. This will keep the young steady too. He wants to be close to anyone who will let Him. No matter their age. To me it's wonderful!

Late in my life I bared myself to Him. He crumbled me and put me back together *His way*. The way I was meant to be in the first place. Everything I held dear or held *to* had to be broken, but as bad as brokenness sounds to people outside of Christ, it isn't bad. It's *essential*. None of what He did in any way lessened me as a human being. It lessened my strain inside. It lessened the burden of running my own life without help. But I'm still the same Ethel in all the ways that were God's ways to begin with. I still have a knocked-out sense of humor. God's humor is terrific! I don't get lonely no more, because Jesus is with me, but I understand the person who is lonely. Way back when I had so much of what the world counts necessary, I was lonely. Now that I have so little, loneliness is *out* because I have so much to be thankful for, and when you're thankful, you can't be lonely, *or* sorry for yourself.

I see elderly people who maybe grew up with a silver spoon in their mouths, but who, in their old age, have *less* and they're miserable. All my life I made a sincere effort *not* to aspire for lofty possessions, heights of any kind except in the quality of my performance. Oh, I expected to be paid for it according to my ability to draw and entertain, but I've always known that when you're on the top, there's no place to go but down. So I've had no trouble recognizing "peace in the valley" now. Mountains are high, a diamond is sparkly and brilliant, but a diamond is cold and so is the air on the top of that mountain. *Cold*. Show business is climbing the mountain and then coming back down. Nobody can stay at the top. Scrambling down to the valley after you've reached the peak doesn't mean you've lost it, that you're no good at your profession anymore. It just means you've been up there and where else can you go?

I like my valley. It's restful here and quiet and I seldom need more than a shawl to protect me from the buffeting winds that sometimes sweep down from that mountain.

Why *should* older people need a lot of money? Jesus promised to look after our needs, to clothe us along with the lilies, to feed us. He *feeds* His sheep. Your big bank accounts are going to be left on earth when you take your flight anyway.

But I wonder if a lot of misery and loneliness among the elderly isn't due to what they call *retirement*? I know I'm blessed to have a profession which can still let me support myself and stay active, but when the day comes that I can't sing no more on a Crusade with Billy or Grady or Leighton or Lane, I don't see why I should consider myself "retired." I can still love, can't I? And love requires action, even if you're sitting in a chair with your feet up.

With Jesus there *is no retirement*. Life *can't* stop when He's around. We're all going to take that one last little breath and leave this earth one day, but if we trust Him, He'll be right there waiting and *life* will go on.

He never goes away while we're on the earth, either. I know now that I'm older and more nervous, I have to fight the fear of being somewhere alone with no one around to help me if I need help. Remember the blackout in the East a few years back? I'd just got into New York City after closing a Crusade with Grady and I wasn't well at all. I was not only so tired I trembled, I just wasn't feeling well and I longed to be able to take a plane straight back to my own home. But I had to stop in New York to take care of some business. Hank Beukema of the Team brought me from the airport to the Empire Hotel and took me up to my room on the eighth floor. Hank had just gone, and because of my weakened condition, I hadn't even unpacked my bags. I was just sitting there by myself in a chair when the lights went out. Well, I thought, surely they'll be back on in a few minutes. So I stayed in the chair, afraid to move around in the dark, afraid I'd fall. Gradually, I began to realize that it wasn't pitch dark anymore! The lights were still off all over the city, but the *moon*—right outside my window—shone so brightly it was like twilight in that room. If you'd wanted to, you could almost read a paper by the light of that full moon. That's what Jesus did for me. I don't say He hung the moon where it was in the sky that night just for me, but I'm His child and He saw to it that I was given a room where the moonlight could get in!

I'm not one to hand out tracts or run up to people to ask them if they're saved. I never have done that, never could do it, never will do it. There are genuine Christians who do and others who abuse such things by overdoing. I love to tell it when He's blessed me or done something especially tender and loving like that moonlight in my room, but it would be artificial to me, phony, to start shoving God at people. Or people at God. He's there. Right there. He can be found as near as a prayer. I don't censure those who make a big show of their faith by leaving tracts under the restaurant bill with the tip. I'm only Ethel and I'm speaking only for Ethel. But God moves into a human heart even through a tiny opening, and my hope and my prayer is that some of those who would be offended by a heavy-handed approach, will just come to understand about His love from my life. Maybe even because I can still laugh! I think people are more curious about Jesus these days. They're thinking about Him more and they want to hear what He can do and what He can mean to someone they *know* didn't always follow Him. My way is just to tell the way it is with me.

Whatever I say here or anywhere all comes out of what I've *lived*. Like my song, "Partners with God," which I wrote with a Jewish boy named Eddie Stewart. He came to me with the music to that song after he'd read a remark I made in an interview right after I began to follow Christ. Now, when you have a big name where the world is concerned, you have to watch. When I decided for Jesus, I was marked. It's hard for people who don't know Him to believe that you won't sell your soul for success. Some writers in particular tried to pressure and embarrass me into taking parts or singing at places I could no longer accept. What they forgot was that the early training I'd had at being a dead-end kid and a street urchin prepared me to tighten my belt. Every so often I'd see or hear about some article on me, insinuating that I was through. Washed up. I once said in an interview, "Look, when you're partners with God, you don't need money!" Well, Eddie Stewart read that piece, brought his music to me in New York, and we collaborated on the song, "Partners with God," which is becoming known now in both Christian circles and the world. But my point is, even that song came out of the fiber of my own life. Experience is what counts.

It's known everywhere I'm known that Ethel Waters belongs to Jesus Christ and sings only for Him. And there is no bond in all of life as strong as the bond between the children of God, but on a human basis, *shared experience* from the past can be helpful, fun, even comforting. My darling child Hal Riddle, to name only one dear friend who once lived in the secular world—Hal and I laugh until we're weak over things that maybe someone who's lived in the shelter of the church all their life wouldn't understand. I don't mean bad things—just funny things that have special associations to those who know the world of the professional theater.

You can joke and laugh with somebody and not offend God, you know. Real humor comes straight from Him! Traveling with the Crusades as I do, naturally I meet all kinds of people, but in my condition and with my energy in such short supply, I try to spend my time when I'm on the road only where it's not going to tire me out too much. Still, you never know where you'll run into someone—man or woman—young or old—who digs you and can be at home with you as quickly and solidly as you can be at home with them. I'm a private person and I don't gush over anybody unless I mean it, so imagine my surprise and my delight when once in Cherryville, North Carolina, with Grady, I met a supporter of the Crusade who was so easy to know, so natural and down-to-earth, I just loved him on sight. His wife too! Those things don't happen often. They really don't. Their names are Buck and Margaret Fraley and, Man! did we hit it off in spite of the differences in our ages.

Buck was friendly and outgoing and I knew he wasn't faking it. Not only was he so wonderful with me, he was the same with everybody. That's the way you can judge a man, you know. Buck doesn't separate people. He was and is just the same with everybody he meets. Why, when my colored people in Cherryville all speak to him on the street or wherever and say "How are you?" like they really want to know, I know Buck's all right.

He was sure all right with me from the start. What I call a good boy. One I felt comfortable with and best of all, I loved and responded to his wife Margaret and the children just the way I did Buck. Almost the first time I talked to him, he confided to me that one of the reasons he loved me so much was that I, in some way, reminded him of his mother, whom he called "Willie Red," who had passed away by the time I met Buck. I knew he was a fine Christian man and, of course, we had that strongest of bonds, along with the fact that I made him think of his mother.

But there's another interesting thing about Buck and me. A plus. Another bond that just adds to what he shared with his mother. She had been a Christian all of Buck's life—and I wasn't! Buck and I were even alike *before* I turned to Christ and oh, boy! for that reason we have a whole lot in common. We can talk to each other on two levels and compare the great peace, fulfillment, and strength that only Jesus can give. Now that I belong to the Lord, I can talk to him the way his mother, Willie Red, always talked and the fact that we both know the old world out there just adds to it. Why, we can laugh at nothing together. He feels free to be himself with me and I feel the same with him. Almost nobody lets you really be yourself. I get a good chuckle just thinking about my darling Buck Fraley. I tell you, we have a ball! You see, Buck's heard the gander sneeze and so have I! *We dig.*

The shocker to all this for me is that I'd known and come to love Buck Fraley and his whole family before I found out that he was a wealthy man. That boy's got to be the most down-to-earth millionaire in the world! He's the president of a whole string of those silver trucks, you know, those big trailer trucks that do all this hauling. Buck's the head of that! I've still got to laugh at myself, because I've met lots of wealthy people in my life, and I just would *never* have guessed that Buck Fraley was one of them. I've been fond of wealthy folks before and respected them. But it was a real surprise about Buck, and by the time I found out that this happy-natured, good fellow had all that money, it was too late for me to go back in my shell! I had no choice but to go on loving him and enjoying him. I really was speechless, though, when I found out. I was stunned and it did me good. You think you know it all and you find out you don't know much.

Buck Fraley understands that my old life is a thing of the past with me. We share both experiences. Life with and without Christ. It helps. It helps.

I don't have to argue and convince somebody like Buck Fraley that when I was in the theater or singing sophisticated club dates, I was doing just what came naturally to me. A lot of people have insisted that I must have had special training in musical styling, in diction. Just because they can understand every word of every song I ever recorded, even back in the old days when they hung one boom mike over both the band *and* the singer, they're sure I had coaching in diction and voice lessons. But people who *dig,* like my babies, Reggie Beane, Buck Fraley, and George Finola *know* I didn't. Not only do I not read music, I never had diction lessons either!

I know you can understand me, that I pronounce every syllable when I sing or speak to an audience. I can flatten my words out when I have to, or when it seems a good idea, or when I'm actin' up, but I've simply spoken clearly all my life. There's no trick and no training. I have no educational background at all. No one taught me to speak or sing this way. You may think the explanation is strange, but the truth is, I have a short tongue.

That's right. A doctor once told me I have a short tongue. I've already told you that the older people used to hit and cuff me due to the space between my teeth, but I have also been punished and slapped and chastised because of the clipped way I speak. To some people, it's clear diction. To my old neighborhood folks, it was impudence. I'm completely unaware of doing it. There's just something in my head that makes me sound every syllable.

There aren't any fancy explanations of my diction any more than of my acting techniques. If I have good diction, it's just that short tongue!

My wonderful Lord has not only caused me to feel loved at last, He has truly given me a new family. A feeling of belonging I've never known before in all the years of my life. It's just plain fun for me to feel free, for example, to call that sweet, adorable Eva Prior in the Atlanta office of the Team—just pick up the telephone and say, "Hello, Eva, baby . . ." To have her come right back with, "Why, hello, Mom!" Jesus has given these children to me in my old age, and they comfort me. These I've mentioned and many, many more. I need them every one. Love like this is teaching me a great lesson. I'm finding it easier to believe now that people do love *me.* That big child who couldn't find a lap large enough to crawl up on, now has almost no shell left around her heart. She's lost almost all her fear of loving. My Lord did this for me. He knew how much love I've always had bottled up inside because I was afraid to pour it all out. Afraid I'd get hurt. Afraid love would slip away. God never does anything in small measure. Now, there are *enough* children for me to love without holding back too much, and they give me great peace and joy.

But Jesus is the only One on whom I can lavish *all* the love I've got. He was the first and He's the *only* One. With Him, I never have to warn myself, "Ethel, be careful. Go slow. You're gonna' be hurt again." People can still hurt me. Jesus never will. I can hurt myself by acting too quick, jumping before I've stopped to listen to His still small voice. Shootin' off with that short tongue. I still do that and before I know it, I've ended up in the wood-shed. But God does *not* put me there! Don't you try to tell me He runs anybody to the woodshed for punishment. We go on our own, by refusing to wait to let Him work things out in His way and at His own pace. God doesn't send hardships to us—you know, the bad things we call His permissive will. It is not God's permissive will that lands me in the woodshed. I'm the one who jumps in myself. I think too fast, act too fast, speak too fast. I keep wanting to put a stopwatch on the Lord. I'm not supposed to do that and I know it. Jumping ahead of Him always lands me in that old woodshed, then when I get in there, I yell, "Lord, lift up the latch, I'm in here!" Don't you let anybody tell you that He sends us there. I *know* I send myself by being too anxious, too impatient, or outspoken, not witnessing as a Christian should.

Sometimes people can all be thinking right about something, some decision they have to make among themselves, say, but they're thinking in different channels—each with his or her own idea to get across—and then somebody gets angry. To this day, just the thought of certain people can make me upset. I confess to that, but I know it's wrong and now I can admit it's wrong. Once in my life I just could *not* openly admit to being wrong about anything, but it's possible because of my precious Saviour. If He let them nail Him to that cross without a word of protest, if He hung there until He died for me—with no anger, with only *love* pouring from the torn places in His body—who am I to fight back?

He's changed me and He's still changing me. He's even changed the meaning of certain parts of the Bible for me. In those old days, when I seemed to live with trouble no matter what, part of the time my own fault and part of the time not, I used to turn to the 71st Psalm for comfort. It articulated my own plea for me. It's still open on my table, just to remind me that this Psalm is no longer my plea. Oh, it held me through some dark days, but it is *no longer* my plea—it is the proof of the *fulfillment* I've found in Jesus Christ. What I mean is that my own heart cry (and don't forget my heart was crying out to God long before I heard Billy Graham preach) was right there in the verses of the 71st Psalm:

In thee, O Lord, do I put my trust: let me never be put to confusion. Deliver me in thy righteousness, and cause me to escape: incline thine ear unto me, and save me.

That cry has been fulfilled. I'm no longer *confused* about how to get back to God. I'm back—safe and sound.

Deliver me, O my God, out of the hand of the wicked, out of the hand of the unrighteous and cruel man. For thou art my hope, O Lord God: thou art my trust from my youth. By thee have I been holden up from the womb: thou art he that took me out of my mother's bowels: my praise shall be continually of thee. I am as a wonder unto many; but thou art my strong refuge.

If you read this book to here, you know what I'm talking about when I say these lines are no longer a heart cry, but a fulfillment. I still stay on the lookout for that "unrighteous and cruel man" but Jesus fell into the hands of unrighteous and cruel men and came out on top! He's not in that grave where they put Him. And I'm in His hands now. I *was* a "wonder," a puzzle, a mystery to my family and to most of my friends. They just didn't understand me, mainly, I guess, because I was afraid to let the real Ethel, the Ethel Waters who longed to love and be loved, come out where they could see her. At age seventy-six, I'm growing up at last on that score. Every day He brings me out a little more and a little more from behind the wall I'd built around myself for what I *thought* was protection.

Now also when I am old and greyheaded, O God, forsake me not; until I have showed thy strength unto this generation, and thy power to every one that is to come. . . . Thou shalt increase my greatness, and comfort me on every side. I will also praise thee with the psaltery, even thy truth, O my God: unto thee will I sing with the harp, O thou Holy One of Israel. My lips shall greatly rejoice when I sing unto thee; and my soul, which thou hast redeemed.

I am "old and greyheaded" now and He has never forsaken me. Singing is all I know how to do, and thanks to my beloved Billy and Grady and Cliff and all the other children in the Crusade, He lets me sing—unto *Him*. The 71st Psalm *was* my heart cry for all those years. Now that heart cry has been fulfilled. *Fulfilled*. When I used to read it and cry in the old days, it was a plea. Now I've received. Then I was seeking. Now I have found. Then I was calling out for delivery. Now deliverance has come.

This big child never knew what it was like to sit on anybody's lap—it's too late for her to find a lap large enough on this earth, but I can laugh about it now and not be bitter, because Jesus is holding this "big child" of His in His arms. His *everlasting* arms.

With me it was my dear Billy, who made it clear from God's Word that I didn't have to do anything special to prove to Jesus I loved Him and wanted to come home. Jesus already knew of my homesickness, but Billy somehow made it clear that all I had to do was *come*. People wonder, I know, when I talk about how much I love and cherish Billy Graham, what would happen to me if (God forbid!) anything happened to Billy. What if, with his brutal schedule and his constant tiredness, the Lord calls him home. You only have to look at him closely and glance at his schedule to know that my child *lives* with exhaustion. But stop your questions, all of you. You miss the point when you wonder about things like that. If my precious child got too tired and went to heaven, I'd go right on because *he* opened God's Word to me and nothing, *nothing* changes that.

One thing I hope and pray for is that *nobody* gets the idea that I came back to Jesus because I was getting old and in a few years would be starting that trip back *down* the mountain whose peak I'd reached in my professional career. I can still make people laugh and cry. At seventy-six, I'm *still* singing on national TV and before larger Crusade audiences than any theater ever held! That's not the point. The point is that I was *tired* living with that flimsy hope some of my children in show business still live with—that rainbow thing had dimmed out for me. When God puts a rainbow in your sky, it stays there. And at the foot of His rainbow is the pure gold of the love and the minute-by-minute *presence* of Jesus Christ —in you. *With you.*

I hope and pray too that some of the church people who read this book will catch on to the fact that God does not have a mold you have to fit. If He did, I'd be sunk. He's there, ready to welcome anybody. Just anybody who really wants to come. He has no favorites—everyone is His special child. I know. I know.

Just before I sang the final number, back when I was still doing my one-woman shows, I think my faith in Him (confused as it was then) and in the life that will go on after we leave this old earth, *showed* in the little ad-lib comment I always made to my audience. It went something like this: "Now my darlings, I would like for you to make me very happy at the conclusion of this performance in carrying this thought—" And then I'd go into "Cabin in the Sky."

To you among my precious children out there in the professional world—or anywhere—just in case we don't have a chance to talk together before Mom goes home, I would like for *you* to make me very happy at the conclusion of this book, in carrying this thought: Jesus Christ can dry your eyes and wipe that unhappy look off your faces. He sees it too, just the way I see it. You don't have to join nothin'—and remember, the only dues to this union with God—is love. I miss you. All of you. *Jesus* misses you. And if you believe in my love for you, just try to think how much He loves you!

Right now, wherever you are, you can turn around and He'll be there *welcoming* you. Waiting to prove His love to you as He's proven His love to Ethel Waters.

A lot of people think the world had the best years of my life. That's not true. With Jesus, every year is the best year of anyone's life. So, therefore, *this* is the best year of my life.

Children, Jesus is real. He loves every "sparrow" *best*. I know, oh, how *I* know. And you will make me very happy if you let me know that by faith you now believe with Mom when she sings . . . To me it's wonderful!

# Editors' Note

Performance highlights in the professional career of Miss Ethel Waters:

After eight years of research, Mr. George Finola of New Orleans has compiled the only known complete discography of Miss Waters' recordings. The remarkable list totals 259, and most of the 259 are now collector's items.

The editors are grateful to George Finola for permission to include this document but regret that it must be reduced to an abridged selection of record titles in combination with roles of major significance in Miss Waters' theatrical biography.

Ethel Waters began singing "for pay" in vaudeville at Baltimore's Lincoln Theater, where she was the first woman to sing (professionally) the classic "St. Louis Blues." Billed later with the Hill Sisters, she toured Negro vaudeville throughout the South as "Sweet Mama Stringbean." In contrast to the huge impassioned styles of Ma Rainey, Sophie Tucker, and Bessie Smith, "Sweet Mama Stringbean" began pioneering an eloquent subtle intimacy. Through the decades, it has remained her trademark.

By the time World War I engulfed America, Miss Waters had played the Lincoln Theater in New York's Harlem and was singing on the regular bill of a club at Fifth Avenue and 132nd Street, Edmund's Cellar, gathering place for top musicians in the twenties. During this period, March 1921, she made her first record (two years prior to Bessie Smith's recording debut). Accompanied by Albury's Blue and Jazz Seven, Miss Waters sang "The New York Glide" (C-673—Cardinal 2036) and "At the New Jump Steady Ball" (C-674—Cardinal 2036). The next two years produced recordings of twenty-six titles for the historic Black Swan label. And she received top billing for the first time in a revue, *Oh Joy!*

Her association with two great arranger-accompanists, Fletcher Henderson and Pearl Wright, is noted on Paramount, Vocalion, and Columbia labels for the succeeding four years. Then she introduced "Dinah" at the Plantation Club on Broadway ("Dinah," 141164-2 Columbia 487-D, Tuesday, October 12, 1925). This hit rocketed her to spectacular success. Between the above date and the spring of 1929, when she immortalized the lament, "Am I Blue?" (148532-2 Columbia 1837-D), Ethel Waters recorded at least forty-seven other titles for Columbia and made her screen debut. The film, the first to be made in "all-color," was *On with the Show.*

But before that milestone, Miss Waters had been acclaimed in the United States and on the Continent; she was already a favorite with the international "society set," and, more significantly, with first-rate instrumentalists. For example, Manny Klein, Tommy Dorsey, Benny Goodman, Adrian Rollini, who cut two sides with her for Columbia in April 1930: "Porgy" (150159-2) and "Black and Blue" (150160-3, both Columbia 2184).

By spring of 1933 she was appearing with Duke Ellington's orchestra at the voguish Cotton Club where she introduced "Stormy Weather," another hit which she recorded repeatedly (13292-a Brunswick 6564, 01524, A-500266, 4842; 36329 Columbia, 2792 LP).

Irving Berlin consequently booked her for his revue *As Thousands Cheer,* which was the most demanding opportunity a Negro woman had been given on "white" Broadway at that time. In this vehicle, Miss Waters proved once and for all her ingenious range of performance, from the ultimate in sophisticated satire and parody, to the electrifying "Heat Wave" and to the unforgettable, anguished "Supper Time." The latter established her as an actress. Oddly enough, there is no recording of "Supper Time" listed until 1947, when she included it along with "Happiness Is Just a Thing Called Joe" for Mary Howard Record, MHR 115. (No catalog number.)

In the late 1930's Ethel Waters, best known for her easy versatility in Broadway comedy revues, accepted the lead role of Hagar in the legitimate play, *Mamba's Daughters.* The interpretation of Hagar, drawn from the torment and stoical courage of her own mother's life, won the praise of the most exacting drama critics. In addition to being one of America's foremost singer-entertainers, Miss Waters was now a ranking actress.

Both talents were ideally combined in the musical, *Cabin in the Sky,* on stage and in the film. Probably the first recording to feature songs from *Cabin* was the one made by Liberty Music Shops in November 1940 ("Taking a Chance on Love," 29031-1, L 310; "Honey in the Honeycomb," 29032-1, L 311; "Cabin in the Sky," 29033-1, L 311; "Love Turned the Light Out," 29034-1, L 310).

Many of the song titles mentioned have been transferred from original discs to Columbia's "Hall of Fame" reissue, *Ethel Waters,* CL 2792. And to Monmouth-Evergreen Records Collector's series, MES/6812. The MES album is "derived" from a taped live performance of Miss Waters' famed one woman shows shortly after her finest artistic success in *The Member of the Wedding* on Broadway (1950) in which she sang, "His Eye Is on the Sparrow."

At the time of this writing, these reissues by Columbia and Monmouth-Evergreen are available, as are the following: Word W-3100, featuring favorite standards for which Ethel Waters is known on the Graham Crusades—"His Eye Is on the Sparrow"; "He's My Rock, My Shield, My Sword"; "Jesus Is Mine"; "Deep River"; "In His Care"; "Just a Closer Walk with Thee"; "I Just Can't Stay Here by Myself"; "Mammy"; "Nobody Knows the Trouble I See"; "He Brought Joy to My Soul"; "Stand by Me"; "When the Trumpet Sounds"; "The Crucifixion"; "I Do, Don't You?"; "Partners with God." Accompanying, the Paul Mickelson Orchestra and Choir; Reginald Beane, piano, on some titles.

Word W-3173, lists "I Am a Pilgrim"; "Sometimes I Feel Like a Motherless Child"; "Here Is One"; "City Called Heaven"; "He's All I Need"; "Choose Now"; "Shall You, Shall I?"; "Little Black Boy"; "Cabin in the Sky"; "He's with Me Each Step of the Way"; "Crying Holy unto the Lord"; "Oh, How I Love Jesus"; "To Me It's Wonderful"; "I Cannot Fail My Lord"; "My Saviour Will Always Be there"; "Is It Well with Your Soul?" Reginald Beane, piano.